LEARNING BUSINESS STRATEGIES

JOHN LOK

First Printing: Dec. 2020

Contents

Preface

Introduction

In our business society, we are facing different kinds of business challenges in different countries business environment. However, in any organizations, staffs and employers also encounter different department difficulties, if we do not know how to find solutions or implement effective strategies to solve these organizational challenges. Our organizations will not achieve raise efficiencies or improve performance. So, if we can predict any kinds of challenges which will be possible to occur as well as we can know how to implement effective strategies to solve these problems. Consequently, we may avoid any challenges occur to cause our organizational failures.

In my this book, I shall attempt to give some opinions to solve any kinds of orgnizational challenges. I shall indicate any business environment challenge and explain the most effective strategies to attempt to solve these challenges. Readers can understand how and why that this kind of strategy which is the most effective solution to this organizational challenge in this organization.

Prologue

Table of content

Climate change how influences global energy need ?
How climate change influences migrant decision to bring economy influence ?
How climate change impacts on developing countries economy ?

Chapter 4 Marketing Strategy How Influences Consumer Behavior
How can Marketing mix strategy solve supermarket store organizational cooperation challenge ? p.76-93
How and why can global human innovation factor influence
China culture and product need change ?
Case study change in the marketing environment on sales of ready meals to supermarket, such as Walt Mark strategy ?

Does Ryanair airline need to concern ecological environment protection strategy ?

How can ethnographic research predict marketing change ?
What are the differences between multi level marketing and direct personal sale?
Chapter 5 How Time Influences Consumer Behavior
Can time pressure influence influence consumer behavior ? p.94-118
How can sellers persuade consumers to choose to buy their products or consume their services in time pressure environment easily?
Can customer purchase experience influence business success?

May time dominate consumption final purchase decision making ?
Is time pressure be the main dominiate to consumer psychological factor ?

How to learning clever shopping consumer mind ?

Can airport time consumption factor influence airport passenger shopping behavior ?

Can web site online internet networking influence traveller individual behavior changes?

What factors influence consumers to shorten time to make choice?
How we can predict or know the consumer time pressure in whom decision making process?

How can sellers persuade consumers to choose to buy their products or consume their services busy environment easily?

How can the brand of product seller influence the supermarket/store fast-moving consumers' more visual attention when the supermarket/store visitor is hurry to make decision to choose to buy which brand of product ?

Can effective advertising can impact of life satisfaction when the consumer feels need to buy the kind of product in any time pressure environment? Can effective advertising bring direct impact on sales when the consumer feels need to buy the kind of product in time pressure environment?

Why does the consumer feel busy or many consumers shopping environment to shorten shopping time ?

Can the consumer make more rational decision , when he/she has enough time to make final purchase decision?

Can busy or many consumers shop environment dominate consumer behaviors?

Why it has relationship between the video game student consumer individual learning time and the working people individual working time both can influence video game playing consumer individual video game choice behavior ?

How can video game advertisement method influence video game softwareconsumer purchase behavior?

Ought salespeople spend long time or short time to explain the product's advantages in order to persuade customers to choose to buy the product more easily?

Can web site online internet networking influence traveller individual behavior changes?

ONE

BEHAVIORAL ECONOMY INFLUENCES CONSUMER BEHAVIOR CHANGE

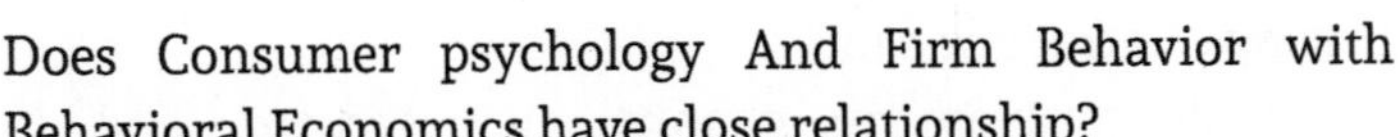

Does Consumer psychology And Firm Behavior with Behavioral Economics have close relationship?

I shall discuss three aspects concern this question to explain how their relationship: economy and customer psychology and marketing Economics and psychology are the two most influential disciplines that underlie marketing. Both disciplines are used to develop models and establish facts, in order to better understand how firms and customers actually behave in markets, and to give advice to managers. While both disciplines have the common goal of understanding human behavior, relatively few marketing studies have integrated ideas from the two disciplines.

We hope that psychologists, who are uncomfortable with broad mathematical models, and suspicious of how much rationality is ordinarily assumed in those models, will appreciate how relatively simple models can capture psychological insight. We also hope that mathematical modelers will appreciate the technical challenges in testing these models and in extending them to use the power of deeper mathematics to generate surprising insights about marketing.

In most applications of utility theory, the attractiveness of a choice alternative depends on only the final outcome that results from that choice. For gambles over money outcomes, utilities are usually defined over final states of wealth (as if different sources of income which are fungible are combined in a single "mental account"). Most psychological judgments of sensations, however, are sensitive to points of reference. This reference-dependence suggests decision makers may care about changes in outcomes as well as the final outcomes themselves.

What does Marketing Application: Business-to-Business Pricing Contracts mean?

A classic problem in channel management (and in industrial organization more generally) is the "channel coordination" or "double marginalization" problem. Suppose an upstream firm (a manufacturer) offers a downstream firm (a retailer) a simple linear price contract, charging a fixed price per unit sold. This simple contract creates a subtle inefficiency: When the manufacturer and the retailer maximize their profits independently, the manufacturer does not account for the externality of its pricing decision on the retailer's profits. If the two firms become vertically integrated and so that in the merged firm the manufacturing division sells to the retailing division using an internal transfer price, the profits of the merged firm would be higher than the total profits of the two separate firms, because the externality becomes internalized.

Standard economic models usually assume that individuals are purely self-interested, that is, they only care about earning the most money for themselves. Self-interest is a useful simplification but is clearly a poor assumption in many cases. Self-interest cannot explain why decision makers seem to care about fairness and equality, are willing to give up money to achieve more equal outcomes, or to punish others for actions which are perceived as selfish or unfair. This type of behavior points to the existence of social preferences, which defines a person's utility as a function of her own payoff and others' payoffs.

Marketing is an applied science that tries to explain and influence how firms and consumers actually behave in markets. Marketing models are usually applications of economic theories. These theories are general and produce precise predictions, but they rely on strong assumptions of rationality of consumers and firms. Theories based on rationality limits could prove similarly general and precise, while grounding theories in psychological plausibility and explaining facts which are puzzles for the standard approach.

Behavioral economics explores the implications of limits of rationality. The goal is to make economic theories more plausible while maintaining formal power and accurate prediction of field data. This review focuses selectively on six types of models used in behavioral economics that can be applied to marketing.

Three of the models generalize consumer preference to allow (1) sensitivity to reference points (and loss-aversion); (2) social preferences toward outcomes of others; and (3) preference for instant gratification (quasi-hyperbolic discounting). The three models are applied to industrial channel bargaining, salesforce compensation, and pricing of virtuous goods such as gym memberships. The other three models generalize the concept of game theoretic equilibrium, allowing decision makers to make mistakes (quantal response equilibrium), encounter limits on the depth of strategic thinking (cognitive hierarchy), and equilibrate by learning from feedback (self-tuning EWA). These are applied to marketing strategy problems involving differentiated products, competitive entry into large and small markets, and low-price guarantees. Thus, base on above factors, I believe that the country's economy development can influence marketing behavior and marketing behavior can influence consumer psychology and behavior. So, they have close relationship.

Behavioral economics studies the effects of psychological, cognitive, emotional, cultural and social factors on the economic decisions of individuals and institutions and how those decisions vary from those implied by classical theory. Behavioral economics is primarily concerned with the bounds of rationality of economic agents. Behavioral models typically integrate insights from psychology, neuroscience and microeconomic theory. The study of behavioral economics includes how market decisions are made and the mechanisms that drive public choice. The three prevalent themes in behavioral economics are.

Behavioral economics is often related with normative

economics. In an ideal world, people would always make optimal decisions that provide them with the greatest benefit and satisfaction. In economics, rational choice theory states that when humans are presented with various options under the conditions of scarcity, they would choose the option that maximizes their individual satisfaction. This theory assumes that people, given their preferences and constraints, are capable of making rational decisions by effectively weighing the costs and benefits of each option available to them. The final decision made will be the best choice for the individual. The rational person has self-control and is unmoved by emotions and external factors and, hence, knows what is best for himself. Alas behavioral economics explains that humans are not rational and are incapable of making good decisions.

Behavioral economics draws on psychology and economics to explore why people sometimes make irrational decisions, and why and how their behavior does not follow the predictions of economic models. Decisions such as how much to pay for a cup of coffee, whether to go to graduate school, whether to pursue a healthy lifestyle, how much to contribute towards retirement, etc. are the sorts of decisions that most people make at some point in their lives. Behavioral economics seeks to explain why an individual decided to go for choice A, instead of choice B.

Because humans are emotional and easily distracted beings, they make decisions that are not in their self-interest. For example, according to the rational choice theory, if one person wants to lose weight and is equipped with information about the number of calories available in each edible product, he will opt only for the food products with minimal calories. Behavioral economics states that even if the person wants to lose weight and sets his mind on eating healthy food going forward, his end behavior will be subject to cognitive bias, emotions, and social influences. If a commercial on TV advertises a brand of ice cream at an attractive price and quotes that all human beings need 2,000 calories a day to function effectively after all, the mouth-watering ice cream image, price, and seemingly valid statistics may lead Charles to fall into the sweet temptation and fall out of the weight loss bandwagon, showing his lack of self-control.

However, when the decision made leads to error, it can lead to cognitive bias. Behavioral game theory, an emergent class of game theory, can also be applied to behavioral economics as game theory runs experiments and analyzes people's decisions to make irrational choices. Another field in which behavioral economics can be applied to is behavioral finance, which seeks to explain why investors make rash decisions when trading in the capital markets.

Companies are increasingly incorporating behavioral economics to increase sales of their products. In 2007, the price of the 8GB iPhone was introduced for $600 and quickly reduced to $400. What if the intrinsic value of the phone was $400 anyway? If Apple introduced the phone for $400, the initial reaction to the price in the smartphone market might have been negative as the phone might be thought to be too pricey. But by introducing the phone at a higher price and bringing it down to $400, consumers believed they were getting a pretty good deal and sales surged for Apple. Also, consider a soap manufacturer who produces the same soap but markets them in two different packages to appeal to multiple target groups. One package advertises the soap for all soap users, the other for consumers with sensitive skin. The latter target would not have purchased the product if the package did not specify that the soap was for sensitive skin. They opt for the soap with the sensitive skin label even though it's the exact same product in the general package.

A cognitive bias (e.g. Ariely, 2008) is a systematic (non-random) error in thinking, in the sense that a judgment deviates from what would be considered desirable from the perspective of accepted norms or correct in terms of formal logic. The application of heuristics is often associated with cognitive biases. Some biases, such as those arising from availability or representativeness, are 'cold' in the sense that they do not reflect a person's motivation and are instead the result of errors in information processing. Other cognitive biases, especially those that have a self-serving function (e.g. overconfidence), are more motivated. Finally, there are also biases that can be motivated or unmotivated, such as confirmation bias (Nickerson, 1998).

As the study of heuristics and biases is a core element of behavioral economics, the psychologist Gerd Gigerenzer has cautioned against the trap of a "bias bias" – the tendency to see biases even when there are none (Gigerenzer, 2018).

As companies begin to understand that their consumers are irrational, an effective way to embed behavioral economics in the company's decision-making policies that concern its internal and external stakeholders may prove to be worthwhile if done properly.

Reference

Ariely, D. (2008). Predictably Irrational. New York: Harper Collins.

Gigerenzer, G. (2018), The bias bias in behavioral economics. Review of Behavioral Economics, 5(3-4), 303-336.

Nickerson, R. S. (1998). Confirmation bias: A ubiquitous

phenomenon in many guises. Review of General Psychology, 2, 175-220.

Can apply the behavioral economic method predict laptop buyer brand choice consumption behavior ?

Think about the last time you purchased a customizable product. Perhaps it was a laptop computer. You may have decided to simplify your decision making by opting for a popular brand or the one you already owned in the past. You may then have visited the manufacturer's website to place your order. But the decision making process did not stop there, as you now had to customize your model by choosing from different product attributes (processing speed, hard drive capacity, screen size, etc.) and you were still uncertain which features you really needed. At this stage, most technology manufacturers will show a base model with options that can be changed according to the buyer's preferences. The way in which these product choices are presented to buyers will influence the final purchases made and illustrates a number of concepts from behavioral economic (BE) theories.

First, the base model shown in the customization engine represents an error preferable choice requirement when any laptop buyer makes his/her laptop decision making choice. It means that when the laptop buyer feels the brand laptop's engine is worse to compare other brands, then he/ she won't choose to buy the brand of laptop. The more uncertain customers are about their decision, the more likely it is that they will go with the preferable error choice requirement , especially if it is explicitly presented as a recommended configuration. Second, the manufacturer can increase or decrease laptop options differently by employing either an 'add' or 'delete' customization mode (or something in between). In an add mode, customers start with a base model and then add more or better options. In a delete option, the opposite process occurs, whereby customers have to deselect options or downgrade from a fully-loaded model. Past research suggests that consumers end up choosing a greater number of features when they are in a delete rather than an add frame or option (Biswas, 2009).

Finally, the option framing strategy will be associated with different price option factor prior to customization, which may influence the perceived value of the product. If the final configured product ends up with a £1500 price tag, its cost is likely to be perceived as more attractive if the initial default configuration was £2000 (fully raising changing price loaded) rather than £1000 (sale price base). Sellers will engage in a process of careful experimentation to find a sweet spot—an option framing strategy that maximizes sales, but set at a default price that deters a minimum of potential buyers from considering a purchase in the first place.Thus, when the laptop brand manufacturers can change to increase or decrease its options , due to their laptop product's feature, function, design, color which are changed, these factors may also excite laptop consumers' buying desires, instead of price reducing and/or engine durable both factors. Because laptop consumers buying desires will not only be influenced by price and engine both factors.

Can apply behavioral Economics method predict exciting Christmas season how influences buyers consumption behaviore?

Some economists dislike Christmas. They allege that it "destroys value," which is, in goes so far as to contend that the winter holiday season is "an orgy of value destruction."

In Christmas, large shopping stores or supermarkets main concern is that the value of gifts to their recipients is typically far lower than the money that was spent on them. Some economists found that of the $65 billion spent on winter holiday gifts in 2009, about 20 percent was wasted in UK supermarkets, in the sense that the gifts were worth that much less to the recipient than they cost. And indeed, it is an inescapable fact of life that people who receive holiday gifts often don't much like what they get. If you've ever been presented with a sweater that you would never wear in public or electronic equipment whose purpose escapes you. Why is present gift one good method to excite supermarkets or superstores consumer buying desires in Christmas season?

In hard economic times, when both the government and ordinary people are trying desperately to save money. We don't propose that Congress should try to solve the debt crisis by requiring people to give holiday season money to the Treasury Department rather than spending it on presents. But misleading -giving does no good for anyone, and we have a few ideas about how to make it through the season a bit more easily. IT HAS PROBABLY already occurred to you that the economic analysis of gift-giving reflects an incomplete understanding of the purpose of gifts, which involve relationships, as well as commodities, and which provide value not only to the recipient but also to the giver. Gifts represent messages—"signals," in social science means giver to recipient. The signals tend to differ for individual givers and receivers, which explains why there are no simple answers to standard how exciting holiday consumption questions, such as whether it is accepted to use present gift to replace cash. Cash is best for some relationships but highly inappropriate for others.

Gifts also serve as investments in relationships. When interpreted this way, the destruction of value can be part of the very essence of gift-giving. If I give you a $20 or 50 gift card for Best Buy and you give me a $20 or 50 e-certificate for Amazon, economists would feel the exchange amount is too less because these amount is not very attractive to exist consumer buying behavior, since no destruction of wealth has occurred. However, very little investment has occurred, either. So, Christmas gift card amount whether it is more or less, it will influence consumer buying desire more or less. Suppose instead that I give you an expensive sweater that you find loathsome, and you give me a fancy travel case for which I have no use. But we will certainly notice the effort and money that went into the purchase. In fact, destroying value in an exchange of overpriced gifts can increase the likelihood that our relationship will endure. If we weren't committed to the relationship, why would we waste the money?

Is gift cards are an extremely attractive method to encourage sale in Christmas season? Behavioral research on perspective-taking provides some explanations for why gift-buying is often such a waste of money. When people try to predict how another person will respond to a certain situation, they begin by imagining how they themselves would respond, and then they make adjustments for differences between themselves and the other person. At both stages, they make big mistakes. Surprisingly, people often make error to predict their own desires. Anyone with unworn clothing in the closet or unread books on the shelf will recognize this problem. One reason we are misled to give to ourselves is that we are creatures of the present. Research on catalog orders finds that, on cold days, people buy warm clothing. However, it takes a few days for the clothing to arrive, and by that time the weather may have changed more warm. This is why the return rate is unusually high for cold-weather products bought in warm temperatures during the cloth buyers buy cloths , the weather is nearly low temperature from high temperature because they feel cooler when the cloths are delivered to their homes in the cooler time.

Luckily, behavioral economics provides some straightforward lessons for gift-givers. Don't assume that other people like what you like. Beware of projecting your current mood onto your purchasing decisions. Avoid unrealistic optimism: People probably won't react as enthusiastically as you expect. Focus on gifts that will get frequent use in Christmas, rather than immediate applause, only to disappear into holiday-season . If you receive a gift card, use it immediately. It is always tempting to save the card for the right moment, which for many cards never comes: Approximately 20 percent of gift cards go unused. If you receive money, do not deposit it in the bank; the moment you do, it will become waste from your savings, because the product price will be possible to raise, if you buy it later. Use it for something you wouldn't have bought otherwise—givers want you to purchase something you'll remember them by.

The good news is that an appreciation of human psychology can make the holiday season not only less expensive, but less stressful and more fun as well. Of course, there are economists who might insist that a maximally efficient holiday season would consist simply of exchanges of cash. So, it has possible that shopping stores can apply gift cards shopping method to encourage consumers to consume more in Christmas season effectively, because many consumers accept to consume more in the year end, it is possible that they won't spend more money to go to travel, so they can save extra much money to consume in themselves countries in preference.

REFERENCE

Biswas, D. (2009). The effects of option framing on consumer choices: Making decisions in rational vs. experiential processing modes. Journal of Consumer Behaviour, 8, 284-299.

Behavioral finance attempts to fill this void by combining scientific insights into cognitive reasoning with conventional economic and financial theory. More specifically, behavioral finance studies different psychological biases that humans possess. These biases, or mental shortcuts, while having their place and purpose in nature, lead to irrational investment decisions. This understanding, at a collective level, gives a clearer explanation of why bubbles and panics occur. Also, investors and portfolio managers have a vested interest in understanding behavioral finance, not only to capitalize on stock and bond market fluctuations but to also be more aware of their own decision-making process.

Behavioral finance encompasses many concepts, but four are key: mental accounting, herd behavior, anchoring, and high self-rating. Mental accounting refers to the propensity for people to allocate money for specific purposes. Herd behavior states that people tend to mimic the financial behaviors of the majority, or herd. Anchoring refers to attaching a spending level to a certain reference, such as spending more money on what is perceived to be a better item of clothing. Lastly, high self-rating refers to a person's tendency to rank him/herself better than others or higher than an average person. For example, an investor may think that he is an investment guru when his investment performs optimally but will dismiss his contributions to an investment performing poorly.

Can apply behavioral economy concept predict share price variation or marketing performance? Behavioral finance is the study of the influence of the psychological factors on financial markets evolution. In other words, financial markets inefficiency is analyzed in the light of the psychological theories and perspectives. Behavioral finance is a relatively recent and high impact paradigm which provides an interesting alternative to classical finance. The classical finance assumes that capital markets are efficient, investors are rational and it's not possible to outperform the market over the long-term. Psychological principles of behavioral finance include among others heuristics and biases, overconfidence, emotion and social forces. A very important step for an investor is to understand his financial personality. In other words, in the posture of investor is vitally important to understand why you make certain financial decisions or how you are likely to react in common conditions of uncertainty. This form of analysis is useful in an attempt to understand how you can temper the irrational components of investment decisions while still satisfying your individual preferences and requirements.
Beyond the rhetorical nuance of the question, obvious financial market imperfections make us wonder if the classical financial theory is not just an unrealistic and incomplete solution to a complex and constantly changing problem. Most of the financial market anomalies cannot be explained using traditional models. Behavioral finance easy explains why the individual has taken a specific decision, but did not find as easily an explanation about how future

decisions will be. Classical finance has as a cornerstone the Efficient Markets Hypothesis, according to whom, since everyone has access to the same information, it is impossible to regularly beat the market, because that stock prices are, in fact, efficient, reflecting everything we know as investors. A market in which prices always “fully reflect” available information is called efficient. Synthesizing, Efficient Markets Hypothesis assume that capital market are informationally efficient.

According to Statman (1999): “Stock market efficiency has two meanings. To some, market efficiency means that there is no systematic way to beat the market. To others, it means that security prices are rational – that is, reflect only “fundamental” or “utilitarian” characteristics, such as risk, but not “psychological” or “value-expressive” characteristics, such as sentiment.” So, in the case of capital markets, the degree of informational efficiency involves the following categories : weak form efficiency, semi-strong form efficiency and strong form efficiency.

In addition, strong form efficiency includes both semi-strong form efficiency and weak form efficiency. Specifically, share prices reflect all information, public and private, but none of these can earn excess returns. In fact, strong form efficiency is the most eloquent example of utopian theoretical construction. In a civilized world, the legal system prevents private information to become public, using various legislative and institutional barriers. Only in a disorganized system which completely ignore legal restrictions could be this possible. Efficient Markets Hypothesis highlight the fact that absolute rationality of the capital market characterized by the fact that all investors are rational it is a statement of fact and must be generally accepted. The question is whether investors can behave in a rational way in the context of an irrational world?

Hence, behavioral finance focuses on the cognitive psychology suggest that the investment decision making process may be analyzed successfully through the following variables : overconfidence, herding complex, overreaction, conservatism, preconceived ideas, excessive optimism, representativeness, irrationality or rational way of thinking and the impact of media channels. Investors can apply behavioral finance concept to attempt to predict when and find reasons why any companies' shares prices change in possible.

The most important issue regarding efficient market theory is that it is not possible to outperform the market over the long-term. An efficient capital market is characterized by the fact that any information is available to all investors or market participants, so stock prices always incorporate and reflect all relevant information. Due to this issue, the price of a stock should reflect the knowledge and expectations of all investors or market participants. It is a certainty that it is not possible to separate an investor's personality and the investment decisions that he may make. Thus, it cannot be ignored the importance of understanding the individual financial behaviour of capital market investors.

Reference

Statman, M. - Behavioral Finance: Past Battles, Future Engagements, Financial Analysts Journal, vol. 55, no. 6 (November/December), 1999, pp. 18-27

Reference

Stigler, G. J. (1950). The development of utility theory. Journal of Political Economy, 58(4), 307-327.

Why environmental protection factor can raise standard of living to bring economic growth ?

In fact, every American community with the problem of balancing environment growth with the need to maintain environmental and social health. For example, efficient agriculture to businesses get information about new technologies to present pollution. Increasing role of quality of life and standard of living took place in countries all over the world, especially nowadays, when numerous affects of the global crisis are felt all over the world. Emerging crisis caused many problems. thereby, in the current situation, it is interesting to examine the level of the quality of life and standard of living. After short overview of general development of concepts of standard of living and quality of life. The different indicators can measure quality of life or standard of living include GDP per capita, shopping basket, GFK basket, households' expenditures, poverty rate, income inequality, life satisfaction and happiness etc. indicators. The measures show an increase in the standard of living and quality of life. Hence, if the result showed the standard of living and quality of life. The high level of human development and the results of the level of satisfaction imply that human are moderately satisfied with their lives and enjoy a rather high level of happiness.

Standard of living and quality of life have been concerning issues in countries for many years, especially nowadays, when numersous effects of the global crisis are felt all over the world. The financial security and prosperity of the economic systems disappeared. The economic storm caused rising unemployment, falling incomes, increasing rates of poverty and declines in overall well-being. Thereby, in the current situation, it is interesting to examine quality of life and standard of living. However, standard of living is defined and the level of welfare available to individual or to the group of people. It concerns products and services, people are able to consume and the recources who have access too. It depends on the quality and quantity of available products and services and the way who are distributed within the population.

Otherwise, standard of living is generally determined by indicators, such as real income per person and poverty rate. Quality of life indicates to the overall welfare within a certain society, focused on enabling each member on opportunity of accomplishing objectives. Unlike the concept of standard of living, quality of life refers to not only indicators of material standard, but also to various subjective factor that influence human lives, such as natural environment pollution challenges. However, in the estimation of standard of living and quality of life their are used two types of measures, objective and subjective indicators. Objective indicators are used to determine and to explain the economic segment, when subjective indicators are used as a descriptive indicator of the noneconomic segment of quality of life and standard of living.

Many researchers were done in the field of economics, psychology, clinical medicine, health care, and social science to measure whether which kind of factors can cause human quality of life to be poor. The understanding of the concepts passed through a long period of evolution. Human need natural resources have enough supply to able to satisfy their needs. It concerns the physical circumstances, such as natural environment in which people live, the products and service who are able to consume and the resources who have access to. So, the good quality of life which depends on the quantity and quality of available products and services and their distribution within the population.

Otherwise, the idea of standard of living requires a macro perspective and it is generally measured by standards, such as real income per person and poverty rate. The most common measure is national output per capita, measured such as GDP or GDP per capita. Other measures, such as income inequality and life satisfaction are also used. So, it can be feeling of human intangible measure, psychological feeling to measure quality of life to human. It seems that the environmental pollution can have close relationship to influence human quality of life. Thus, quality of life can be measured by objective as well as subjective indicators. One researcher, Felce and Perry (1995) who defined quality of life is as total welfare which includes objective and subjective evaluation of physical, material, social and emotional welfare, personal development and activity, all together evaluated throughout personal set of values.

What are objective indicators of standard of living and quality of life? Objective circumstances refer to the economic and material conditions which are important aspects of the standard of living and quality of life. In the assessment, eight different indicators were used: CPI, GDP per capita, shopping basket, household's expenditures, GFIC basket, poverty rate, income inequality and HDI. However, these indicators is one number measure. It can't measure anyone's psychological feeling, such as health, safe emotion. The challenge concerns whether environmental pollution factor, such as air pollution, water pollution can cause human's health to be poor, even goes down human's quality of life and economy loss. I shall indicate some evidences to give reasons to support my conclusion why I believe that environment pollution is a factor to cause human quality of life to be poor , even it can also cause economy will encounter loss too.

In general, measure of quality of life need include human's psychological feeling indicator. I shall indicate, Hong Kong, China countries air and water environmental pollution challenges how to influence these two countries' people quality of life to be poor, even, it will cause their economy loss. Nowadays, China and Hong Kong and India and Africa are encountering health problems arising from damage to lungs, heart and blood vessels. Hong Kong and India and Africa and China e.g. Shanghai city pollution is a significant cause of premature death from cardiopulmonary disorders. Present level of pollution cause injury to the immature developing lings of children and adolescents. This damage will lead to life-long health problems in many and a reduction in life-expectancy. Although, there is no evidence from analyses of trends in pollutants that pollution measures in recent years have reduced pollutant concentrations in a way which will benefits public health.

There are clear indicators that for some pollutants. The problem is worsening. In fact, air and water pollution is Hong Kong and China and Africa etc. developing countries' the biggest cause of social and environmental injustice. It harms not only citizens today, but because its trans qenerational effects on the unborn and youngest members of the society, it will cause its will health effects well into the later years of this century, even environmental pollution challenge will cause these countries will encounter economy loss.

Human activities have created forms of air and water pollution, such as gases from fuels, uncontrolled emissions from fossil fuels and other chemical sources have long been recognized as a cause of ill health and premature death. For example, in December, 1930 year, a dense fog affected the Meuse Valley in Belgium. Beginning on December, 3 date, the fog intensified over three days and was associated with laryngeal symptoms, chest pain, coughing, and breathlessness. Some patients showed signs of pulmonary oedema. Overall 60 deaths were attributed to the episode. After a long investigation, the cause was considered to be emissions from high sulphur fuels, including suplhur dioxide and sulphuric acid.

What is the current threat to health? the migration of air pollution following the introduction of clear air has been followed by a period of unprecedented economic development creating new forms of pollution from the combustion of fossil fuels. For example, in contrast to the relatively large tar laden particulates from burning dirty coal which caused episodes like the London city, UK. Smog , traffic pollution now generates fine with a different size and composition and gases, such as which may cause injury to the respiratory system and the effects of other pollutants. Such as particulates and drive the formation of the secondary pollutant ozone. The effects of pollution will therefore to some extent reflect genetic, environmental lifestyle and behavioral factors to develop these distance in a population together with the existing prevalence of diseases which may be polluted.

Hence, living in polluted urban environments is associated with increased levels of biological markers of inflammation compared with residence in a clean air environment. The damage is caused by air pollution manifests itself through a variety of common and recognized health problems, such as upper complaints heart and lung disease. Because of this, we can use statistical methods as well as clinical studies to detect the signal of changes in health problems and increased health care demands in the population. However, doctors had proved air or water pollution can cause these both curdiovscular or respiratory disease indirectly. Curdiovscular disease includes formation of arterial plaques, coronary artery, heart attacks, irregular heart rhythm, loss of heart rate variability, high blood pressure, stroke etc. disease. Respiratory disease includes inflammation of nasal, throat and tracheal airways with acute, lower respiratory tract inflammation and infection causing bronchitis, reduction long growth and function in young people. So, it seems environmental pollution can influence quality of life to human as well as environmental pollution and illness and poor health problem has close relationship.

On the other side, environmental pollution can bring health risk, over it will influence social inequalities. Some researchers had found that the evidence has been compiled for six environmental health challenges, such as air quality, housing and residential location, unintentional injuries in children, work related health risks, waste management and climate change. It seems human need to concern air and drinking water quality, waste management and climate change how to influence our environmental pollution challenge. Although, the evidence base on social inequalities and environmental risk is fragmented and data are often available for few countries only, it indicates that inequalities are a major challenge for environmental health policies. Irrespective of development status, environmental inequalities can be found in any country for which data are available. The valid for the exposure to environmental risk factor is also unequally distributed, and this unequal distribution is often related to social characteristics, such as income, social status, employment and education, even environment risk factor can influence human's quality of life.

Why does environment pollution can brings proverty in poor economy?

In fact, environment pollution and human right abuses has close relationship. It is clear that poverty situations and human rights abuses are worsened by environmental degradation. The result can influence poor human quality of life to the developing countries' people unfairly. There are these several obvious reasons: firstly, the exhaustion of natural resources leads to unemployment and emigration to cities; secondly, this affects the enjoyment and exercise of basic human rights. Environmental conditions contribute to a large extents to the spread of infections diseases. From the 4,400 million of people who live in developing countries, almost 60% lack basis health care services, a almost a third of these people have no access to safe water supply; thirdly, degradation poses new problems, such as environmental refugees. Environmental refugees suffer from significant economic, socio-cultural and political consequences. And fourthly, environmental degradation worsens existing problems suffered by developing and developed countries. David J. Nowak & Gordon M. Melsler (2016) showed" Air pollution , for example, accounts for 2.7 million to 3.0 million of deaths annually and of these 90% are from developing countries. " Hence, our societies need to concern human right law to protect unfair treatment to developing countries people. Firstly, both disciplines have deep social root, even though human rights law is more rooted within the collective consciousness, the accelerated process of environmental degradation is generating a new " environmental consciousness". Secondly, both disciplines have become internationalized . The international community has assumed the commitment to observe the realization at human rights and respect for the environment. Thirdly, both areas of law tend to universalize their object of protection. Human rights are presented as universal and the protection of the environment appears as everyone is responsibility.

Human right and environment law can raise our quality of life because the first approach is one where environmental protection is described as a possible means of human rights standards. Here, environmental law is conceptualized as giving a protection that would help ensure the well-being of future generations as well as the survival of those who depend immediately upon natural resources for their livelihood. So, the end is human rights, and the route is though environmental law, the second approach places the two sphere in inverted positions, it states that the legal protection of human rights is an effective means to achieving the ends of conservation and environmental protection. Therefore, the presently existing human right is as a route to environmental protection. The focus is on the connection to influence any economy: health, food supply , housing, fresh natural air supply etc. aspects of quality of life issues. Hence, human right and environment law and human quality of life and economic growth has close relationship . We can not neglect to concern how to achieve human right law to protect our nature environment existing in our societies.

What are environmental factors affect human health in important way, both positive and negative? On positive environmental factor aspect, which can sustain health, and promoting them is preventive medicine. They include : sources of nutrition (farming, oil quality, water availability, bio diversity/bio integrity, genetically modified organisms ; hurting, fishing: wildlife, fish populations; water (drinking, cooking, cleaning, sanitation); air quality; ozone layer (protection from cancers disease etc.).; space for exercise and recreation, sanitation/waste recycling and disposal. On negative environmental factors aspect, which are threats to health, and controlling them is public environmental health. They include: environmental conditions disease sectors (endemic and exotic sectors); invasive biota (bacteria etc.), their hosts and sectors; environmental disruptions: floods, droughts, storms, fires earthquakes, volcanoes; air quality: pollution landing to respiratory disease or cancers; water quality: biotic and abiotic contaminants ; integrity of water transport and structure; monitoring and management of municipal, agricultural, industrial outflows to the environment (gases, liquids, solid waste), human changes of the environment that: create conditions that favour disease; disturb and release noxious levels of previously bound chemicals (e.g. mercury released becomes poison) or bioto (e.g. methane released from thawed peat contributes to climate changes, create temporary, intense, life threatening heat islands (e.g. urban heat waves exacerbated by climate change); result from nuclear; biological or chemical welfare or terrorism, disruption cased by other war and violence.

How and why pollution influences nutrition, and health to bring death disease to decrease consumer desires and economic recession in the polluted country? In consumer view point, any one food consumer must consider his health, he will feel fear to buy any dirty foods to eat. So , although the food price is cheaper , but if he feels the food is not fresh. Then, he will refuse to choose to buy the kind of food to eat. So, one dirty food market will influence food consumers feel fear to get illness and it will influence many food buyers do not stay long time in the direty food

market, even it can cause they refuse to enter the dirty food market because they feel the dirty food market may bring any new kinds of illness when they contact the dirty food (death animal bodies or the food sellers who may get any kinds of new illness when they need to contact the dead of animals, due to they need to kill them often). SO, they will have possible to get illness from the dirty animals, e.g. pig, cow bodies. It's often said that one man's junk is another man's treasure, such is the perception of value in product development and marketing. So many factors influence our perceptions and
they can change over time and alter consumer behaviour.

Vouchercloud's recent "Perception of Values" data graphic delves into this further, looking at the psychology behind our perception of value and examines trends, marketing practices, different generation's attitudes towards value and other factors. Some of the specific areas that the data covers are:

TWO

E-Commerce Marketing How Influences Consumer Behavior CHANGE

E-commerce how influences consumer behavioral changes to bring positive or better economy growth to the country?I shall explain how e-commerce consumer behavior influences the country's economic growth or recession, they have direct case and effect relationship as below: How can consumer e-commerce consumption behavior bring the economic impact of e-commerce ? E-commerce has altered the practice, timing, and technology of B2B and B2C markets, affecting everything from transportation patterns to consumer behavior. The development of electronic commerce, the most basic of economic transactions— the buying and selling of goods—continues to undergo changes that will have a profound impact on the way companies manage their supply chains. Simply put, e-commerce has altered the practice, timing, and technology of business-to-business (B2B) and business-to-consumer (B2C) commerce. It has affected pricing, product availability, transportation patterns, and consumer behavior in developed economies worldwide.

B2B e-commerce leads the way

Business-to-business electronic commerce accounts for the vast majority of total e-commerce sales and plays a leading role in global supply chain networks . In 2003, approximately 21 percent of manufacturing sales and 14.6 percent of wholesale sales in the United States were e-commerce related; by 2008 those percentages had increased to almost 40 percent for manufacturing and 16.3 percent for wholesale trade. One reason why B2B e-commerce is more sophisticated and larger in size than direct to- consumer e-commerce is that B2B transactions developed out of the electronic data interchange (EDI) networks of the 1970s and 1980s. The steady growth in business-to-business e-commerce has changed the cost and profit picture for companies worldwide. At the microeconomic level, growth of B2B e-commerce results in a substantial reduction in transaction costs, improved supply chain management, and reduced costs for domestic and global sourcing. At the macroeconomic level, strong growth of B2B e-commerce places downward pressure on inflation and increases productivity, profit margins, and competitiveness.

Double-digit growth for B2C

E-commerce retail has become the fastest growing trade sector and has outpaced every other trade and manufacturing sector since 1999, when the U.S. Census Bureau started collecting and publishing data on e-commerce. That year, e-commerce retail sales represented less than 1 percent of total U.S. retail sales. In 2003 that number climbed to a little less than 2 percent; by 2008 it had grown to 3.6 percent, and by the fourth quarter of 2010 B2C e-commerce reached 4.4 percent of total U.S. retail sales. In dollar terms, e-commerce retail revenue currently stands at approximately US $165 billion, considerably less than the US $3.9 trillion that represents the total U.S. retail market. During the "Great Recession," which lasted from December 2007 through June 2009, manufacturing, wholesale, and bricks-and-mortar retail sales took a heavy beating. By the fourth quarter of 2010 they still had not fully recovered, even though U.S. gross domestic product (GDP) and personal spending (adjusted for inflation) had surpassed their previous peaks seen in late 2007.

Retail e-commerce, by contrast, weathered the recession relatively well, albeit with considerably slower growth than had been seen prior to the financial crisis. In the first quarter of 2002, retail ecommerce experienced quarterly, year-over-year growth of about 42 percent. On the eve of the recession, that rate dropped to a still-respectable 18 percent. Quarterly sales continued to grow until the latter part of 2008, and in the fourth quarter of 2009 sales surpassed the previous peak. It's important to note here that a large portion of B2C sales come through mail-order houses, many of which have an online presence as well as traditional storefront outlets. Contrary to popular opinion, mail-order houses still have a very strong online presence, and until just recently their sales outperformed online-only retailers. How e-commerce influence the country's economic and consumer behavioral changes ? The changes that B2C e-commerce has sparked arguably have had a more significant impact on the economy and on buyers' behavior than has B2B ecommerce. In the past, when consumers wanted to make purchases they had to set aside time to shop during certain hours of the day, or they had to read through catalogs sent to them by mail-order houses. Today, many consumers can simply use their computers— and now smart phones or other portable electronic devices—to shop online. Buyers and sellers that engage in e-commerce retail trade are no longer restricted by store hours, geographic marketing areas, or catalog mailing lists. With a few simple clicks they can gain access to a variety of goods 24 hours a day, seven days a week.

The characteristics of retail e-commerce merchandise also have changed significantly over the past decade. Back in 2000, computer hardware was the most common type of merchandise sold over the Internet. Today, the variety of merchandise is extremely diverse, and shoppers can buy almost anything online. Online shoppers have benefited in other ways. The growth of e-commerce retail sales has reduced consumers' search cost, placed downward pressure on many consumer prices, and reduced price dispersion for many consumer goods. But this has led to a substantial decrease in the number of small companies operating in certain industries, as they tend to be less involved with e-commerce. Larger businesses, most notably retail book outlets, new automobile dealerships, and travel agents, are better able to compete in this new market environment.

The extremely rapid growth of e-commerce retail sales has provided a major boost to residential parcel delivery services. That's because online merchandise purchases involve some form of residential delivery by a third-party vendor such as FedEx, UPS, or the U.S. Postal Service. In addition, there appear to be considerable synergies related to B2C parcel and heavier freight volumes—parcel industry insiders have observed that businesses with strong e-commerce related B2C parcel shipment volumes often have stronger B2B shipment volumes than those that do not engage in B2C e-commerce.

How the E-commerce influences demand patterns ? As technology, e-commerce, and globalization become more intertwined, buyers and sellers are increasing their connectivity and the speed with which they conduct sales transactions. As we saw during the recent turmoil in the financial markets and some supply chain networks, speeding up sales transactions can be a very positive attribute when small market corrections are taking place. However, during a major economic correction like the one we witnessed during the Great Recession, a quicker response to sales transactions can have cascading impacts on supply chains, resulting in large contractions or expansions in orders, production, shipments, and inventory. Thus, there are some potentially negative consequences to the rapid growth of e-commerce. In this volatile business environment, supply chain managers should consider developing strategies for dealing with the rapid swings that can result from increasing use of e-commerce in a globalized market.

In conclusion, the high technological e-commerce online shopping model change, it can influence consumer behavior change to influence any country's economic environment to change to be better or worse. So, they has direct relationship between the country e-commerce development and its economic recession or growth. The impact of e-commerce and R&D and two other variables on economy development in 21 selected countries. This study used panel data technique with Generalized Least Square Regression (GLS) method during the period of 2005 to 2013. The results showed that e-commerce and R&D had a positive and significant impact on GDP (Gross Domestic Product) per capita based on purchasing power parity, with e-commerce having a stronger development-enhancing effect in comparison to R&D. Health expenditure and government size as other dependent variables also had a positive influence on GDP per capita, which could be effective in improving and growing the economy.

REFERENCE

Biswas, D. (2009). The effects of option framing on consumer choices: Making decisions in rational vs. experiential processing modes. Journal of Consumer Behaviour, 8, 284-299.

Factors Influencing E-Commerce Development Implications for the Developing Country consumer behavior ? The availability and continued growth of Internet technologies (IT) have created great opportunities for users all over the globe to benefit from IT services and use them in a variety of different ways. The use of IT to conduct business online is known as Electronic Commerce (E-Commerce). We are witnessing a boom of new technologies, especially in the service sector (IT, Telecommunications, Internet, etc.). Due to technological advances economic transactions have become much easier and faster and this is mainly because of the development of e-commerce. Real engine of the new economy, e-commerce is a remarkable source of competitive advantage for businesses and a new space for consumers. In the coming years, growth and profitability will depend most likely the ability to introduce these new emerging technologies and adopt new methods of business transactions. Since many years ago computers, appliances, plane tickets and many other items are available for purchase on the Internet using cards issued by local banks. Although this technological trend could significantly strengthen the national economic structure, its role and place in developing countries economic structure remains unclear and leaves many questions to ask:

Why does consumers need e-commerce in developing countries? What are the obstacles to e-commerce? Is e-commerce having a bright future to become a mainstream business for growth, and what steps to take to get there? While developed countries have harnessed and adopted E-Commerce, developing countries are not yet fully adapted to its adoption. The aim of this study is to investigate the factors that play a role in the adoption and development of E-Commerce and, hence, develop strategies that conceptualize the influential factors that form as enablers and disablers of E-Commerce. In this paper we provide some answers about the current situation of e-commerce think later on prospects that will enable the benefits from all the advantages offered by this new mode of trade. This paper is organized as follows. Firstly, a concept of e-commerce is briefly introduced, followed by the construction of the research model, including all the aspects of e-commerce that are the object of our investigation. Finally, implications drawn on the study results and analysis are discussed, followed by the research limitations and a conclusion. factors influencing e-commerce. The factor may include as below to influence

developing countries customer behavioral change :
What are Implications for Ecommerce in Developing Countries consumer ?Shopping convenient need factor ? In developing countries, IT and communication or rather e-commerce growth are substantial. Technology effectiveness is essential in E-Commerce success. However, human, economic, and other organizational issues must be taken into account as well. In this study, we evaluated the current status of E-Commerce in Developing countries. The evaluation of current status reveals opportunities that should be seriously tackled by organizations, if they are to survive the consequences of globalization and open markets. There should be an immediate implementation of a governmental infrastructure to support e-commerce. This thesis explored the areas enabling and huddles to the development of e-commerce. Online consumers face problems concerning security and privacy. They are exposed with online risk such as hacker mischiefs. Moreover, when buyers make payment using credit cards, they are exposing their banking information which could also be manipulated by hackers. The results of this research showed that majority of the respondents felt that internet shopping is risky due to the same reason. Amongst the perceived risks is financial, product performance, social, psychological and time convenience loss. Other than stolen credit card information, there are also risks in delivery. The time taken for delivery may take quite some time, therefore, anything could happen in the process of delivery. Buyers may lose the item. Online vendors might not be responsible for the loss and this leaves the buyers to bear all the consequence. When the perceived risk is greater, the relationship between intention and online purchasing will be weakened.

- Accessibility and Awareness factor

The perception of user interface quality and the degree of awareness on information about products and services delivered from conducting transactions from any location at any time through e-commerce portals. factors

- Quality and benefits factor

The perception of quality of products and services offered from e-commerce portals and benefits that arose from conducting such transactions.

In conclusion, Countries need to encourage and improve the e-commerce developments. This research sheds light on the potential factors that may play a significant role in supporting the proliferation and advancement of E-Commerce in developing countries. The outcomes of this study may contribute to the market stakeholders' understanding of their potential customers' needs and current concerns. Exploring the market, especially at this time while e-commerce is still in its development stage, is critical for industry stakeholders in order to ensure the success of this emerging market. Future research should focus on studying the development of e-commerce and testing the research model. Consequently, potentially important dimensions of the study could include an investigation in multiple cities, and especially in more rural areas, which may lead to more accurate and comprehensive results and analysis. Also, comparative research in different parts of the world would produce more complete findings. The results of this study could then be compared with those of other developing countries having similar conditions to see if there is a significant difference.

Reference

?Miyazaki, A. D., & Fernandez, A. (2000). Internet privacy

and security: An examination of online retailer disclosures. Journal of Public Policy & Marketing, 19(1), 54-61, CrossRef

THREE

Climate How Influences Consumer Behavior Change

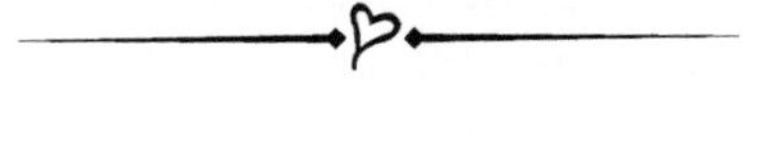

How immigration influences economy ? What are immigration impacts to social econoomy? Immigration how influences into a region impacts house prices in three ways. For a fixed level of local population, housing demand rises due to the increase in foreign-born population. In addition, immigrants can influence native location decisions and induce additional shifts in house demand. Does immigration cause housing prices to be higher ? In applied economic view, economists determined that illigration contributed to no more than 0.1% to 0.12% increase in housing prices. Furthermore, an increase in new

housing construction in response to higher demand also moderated the effect of immigration.
What impact did immigration have on society? The available evidence suggests that immigration leads to more innovation, in better educated workforce, greater occupational specialization, better working of skills with jobs, and higher overall economic productivity. Immigration also has a not positive effect on combined local budgets.How does overpopulation affect housing by increasing immigrant number? Population change leads to a changing demand for housing population growth, and particularly the growth in the number of housing population growth, and particularly the growth in the number of households leads to a growth in hosing demand. Population decline might in the long term, leads to a decrease in housing demand.

However, immigration also brings good aspect to economy, instead of netagive aspect. The available evidence suggests that immigration leads to more innovation, a better educated workforce, greater occupational specialization, better matching of skills with jobs, and higher overall economic productivity. Immigration boosts the well-being of the society. If the growth rate of per-capita income increases thanks to immigrants, the standard of living of the general population can rise. For canada exampls, immigration can bring positive impact to Canada's economy. The 2026 census found that immigrants had median earnings of $29,770 compared to $36,300 for native born Canadians. Recent immigrants are far more likely than native born canadians to initially have low incomes, with income and employment rates increasing towards the national average with more than spent in canada.What are the positive or negative impact to immigration? The channels have both positive and negative static and dynamic effects. One netagive static effect of immigration is that migration directly reduces the available supply of labour, particularly skilled labour, but these are positive static effects , such as through return migration and remittances.

The positive impacts of migration may include the opportunity to get a better job, improved quality of life, safety from conflict. The opportunity of a better education. The negative impacts of migration may include: Poverty makes them unable to live a normal and healthy life. Children growing up in pvoerty have no access to proper nutrition, education or health. Migration increased the slum areas in cities which increase many problems, such as unhygienic conditions, crime, pollution etc. How does migration affect the economy in global? The available evidence suggests that immigration leads to more innovation, a better educated workforce, greater occupational specialization, better matching of skills with jobs, and higher overall economic productivity. Moreover, immigration also have has a not positive effect on improving productivity to the country's manufacturers aspect, for example, labour migrants have the most positive impacts on either positive or negative terms. The impact is negative, it brings small impact of the human capital brought by migrants on skillful manufacturing jobs aspect. As the same time, emigration can have a positive impact on development. Positive impacts on host countries, reducing job vacancies number and improving skills by overseas skillful immigrants. Also, returning migrants can bring savings, skills and international contacts.

Hence, the economic effects of migration, it indicates that high skilled migrants bring diverse talent and expertise, when foolish or poor skillful workers are improved or upgrade high skill and has no negative efffects on public fiances as immigration is found to have an overall positive impact on economic growth in long term. Moreover, the positive impact not just on population growth. Many migrants bring higher education and skill. The expanded attributed allow the modeling to better capture both the positive and negative impacts.

On conclusion, migrants have positive impact on developing countries called " how immigrants contribute to developing countries economies, e.g. leading a greater cultural diversity, social benefits, raising economic costs to manufacturers, e.g. reducing manufacturing cost, assisting refugees , e.g. households wealth, increasing due to they can find jobs to do easily when they emmigrate to the another country, such as migrant workers are an aset to the country where they bring their knowledge and skill to attribute to the new country's society. Hence, I think that immigration can bring many advantages to a country both for the economy and society as a whole.

Does health reason influence developing countries people to choose migration by climate change impact? Climate change is caused substantial increases in population movement. It has considered the likely causal influences much movement and the risks to national and international security. But, there has been little research on the consequences of climate-related migration and the health of people who move. May health impacts of climate change play important role in population movement?
However, climate change-related migration is likely to result in adverse health outcomes, particularly in situations of forced migration. In fact, climate change is widely

projected to cause substantial increases in the scale of human population movement. Forecasts of the number of people who will move by around midcentury in response to the effects of climate change vary from tens of millions to 250 million people (United Nations High Commissions For Refugees (UNHCR, 2009).

Many scientists believe migration reason is common that the countries' people are fear of diseases and climate change environmental disasters to be caused in their countries, especially developing countries by climate change negative influences. Specially, populations in low-income countries whose health is most at risk from climate changes and where. There are often high pre-existing levels of health problems are used to coping with adverse health outcomes without causing to migration. So, it is likely that population movement that is driven substantially by health risks will occur only where those risks are sufficiently serious and widespread. For example, Africa the country's climate change will bring the risk of infectious disease (e.g. cholera , measles, malaria, meningitis) to Africa. In fact, Africa has adequate health care systems, low immunization coverage, lack of clean water and poor sanitation (Zarocostas, 2011). Thus, it seems that climate change will bring health rick challenge to the country to influence people to choose to migrate other countries. Although, the range and extent of health risks with future climate related population movements can't be clearly forever, but the evidence of health outcomes of movement of people indicates that health risks will predominate over health benefits. This often is an issue of considerable geopolitical, ethical and economic importance. Consequently, it has close cause and effect relationship between climate change and health risk to cause people to choose migration.

Impact of population growth and population ethics on climate change mitigation

Future population growth migration number is uncertain, due to climate change factor influence. Higher mitigation growth entails more emissions and means either more people will choose to mitigate other better climate countries to live or the better climate countries will have more people to immigrate to live, due to any sudden climate change environment related impacts. However, some climate scientists feel how future population is related importantly determines mitigation decisions. They indicated that some bad climate countries' people make any mitigation decision choice, it responds to the fact that a larger population means climate change hurts more people. For example, in 2025 year assuming United Nations has high rather than low population scenario entails an increase in the social cost of carbon dioxide (SCC) of 85% under total utilitarianism (TU), vs 5% under average utilitarianism (AU). The difference is the (SCC) between the two population scenarios under (TU) is comparable to commonly debated decisions regarding time discounting. Additionally, they estimate the avoided mitigation costs implied by reductions in population growth, finding that large neat term savings US $6billions amount annually occur under (TU). Hence, it seems that climate changing is one important factor to bring any bad climate change countries which need to pay large disaster expenditure to recover their economy after any sudden serious climate change impacts.

How climate change impacts on developing countries economy ?

In fact, climate change will increase global temperature change rainfall patterns and will result in more frequent and severe floods and drought. Depending on future emission of greenhouse gases, global temperatures are likely to rise between 2 degree and 4 degree within the next century. The main impacts of climate change will however not be felt through higher temperatures, but through a change in the hydrological cycle. Rainfall is likely to increase around the poles and the tropics when in the sub-tropics average precipitation is likely to decrease. Not only the average annual or seasonal rainfall will change, there also be an increase in the number of extreme events resulting in most frequent and severe floods and droughts. How does climate change influence to development countries? Climate change will influence any development countries on these several aspects. They include as below:

On trade influence hand, reducing emission levels from the developing world is extremely important. If current developments are continuing, for example, emissions from China and India both countries will save be much higher than the total emission form all Europe countries. Currently, the Europe is stimulating mitigation and transfer of clean technologies through the clean development mechanism (CDM). Although, it is still unclear what the mitigation potential of the (CDM) is, especially in India the investment is (CDM) projects is significant. However, the Europe should take a much wider approach. In developing countries a lot can be done in terms of increasing energy efficiency, land use change and agriculture. It is also important that developing countries are stimulated to choose a sustainable, low emission developed pathway. Choices for more sustainable, low emission technologies should be made early in the process. It seems that climate changing will encourage many countries will choose to do more environment protection related trading, e.g.

researching how to invent environment protection new products to reduce our earth pollution between European and any developing countries, such as China and India etc.

On focus mitigation efforts in least developed countries on land use change, agriculture development aspect, in the least developed countries mitigation efforts should not focus on the energy or transport sector, but on agriculture and forestry. Agriculture is responsible for a relatively large percentage of the emissions in many developing countries, e.g. Africa, China, Malaysia, Hong Kong, Japan etc. In this sector there are many win options both reducing poverty and reducing greenhouse gas emissions. For example, improved water and nutrient management can sharply increase production efficiency and reduces at least the amount of emission per kg food produced. Agro-forestry reduces greenhouse gas emission through increased carbon storage and reduces poverty through diversifying the incomes of local communities.

However, in most developing countries, the main limitation in coping with the impacts of climate change is a lack of capacity. Besides a lack of capacity, in many developing countries, there is also a significant lack of data and knowledge on climate change impacts. Developing countries should be stimulated to improve data gathering and make existing data more easily available.However, no migration effort will stop the need for adaptation. Especially, the least developed countries, who have contributed little to the problem will suffer the most. On business strategies for climate change aspect, nowadays, the valuation for clean-technology companies, have increased considerable and the corporate carbon footprint has become an important topic to be discussed how to solve among senior managers? How can firms profit from what they do to address climate change? Thus, a low-carbon economy is already especially in energy, transport and heavy industry. If current climate science holds true and there is considerable uncertainty in the estimates, global greenhouse gas emissions should ideally decrease from today's levels by 90 percent as of 2050 year in order to certain global warming below two degrees centigrade. Hence, it seems global warmth challenge brings further any new energy potential development businesses. Due to environment scientists encourage us to be realized the necessary increase in carbon productivity and new low-carbon technologies that are necessary dramatically reduces energy consumption and direct greenhouse gas emissions will have to be developed and then implemented widely to avoid future serious global environment warmth caused climate changes and pollution challenges occurrence.

What are the cause and effect economy relationship between climate change and environment migration ? The choice of migration reasons can include that seeking better job chance, better job environment, better salary, better standard of life, better education, less crimes, feeling more safety etc. different psychological reasons. However, whether climate changing will be one factor to cause migration. This is one psychological life adaption issue. Some people may accept to adapt to live worse life when their countries are encountering any natural environment or economic negative or climate negative change or social negative impact suddenly. Otherwise, some people may not accept to adapt to live worse life when they countries are encountering any worse influences suddenly, such as sudden worse climate change. Thus, to research that whether it has relationship to influence migration choice between climate change and migration. We need to know whether what the general acceptable level to adapt climate change to human is. It means that if the climate change has exceeded the countries' general people's acceptable level to adapt to live in their countries. Then, it is possible that it will cause many people do not feel more adaptive to live in their countries forever, due to serious sudden climate change disaster occurrence.

What is the general acceptable level to live to their countries to adaptive climate change? However, before they choose to migrate, they will mind these questions usually. How can they migrate? Once they leave, who will guard their land? How will they support their family in the city? Environment problems are both sudden and gradual have always causal different formed of displacement around the world, but recent studied have emphasized that more people are likely to migrate in the future, owing to climate change (Stern, N. 2007).

In fact, climate change will bring serious challenge to any countries, such as natural resources shortage, lacking more productive livelihoods supply. Then, it views this question: If migration have no adaptive potential, then what can be done (or is being done) to facilitate communities to migrate? Analyzing who migrants, how, why and where they go can provide useful insights for development planners aiming to support poor families. It seems that every family member's adaptive to live factor will influence the whole family who decides to choose to migrate or stay in their country when climate change disaster sudden occurs. However, environmental migration is typically internal and short term, the potential for conflict is that unstable urban and rural demographics are related to higher risks of civil war and low level conflicts to environment migration during periods of environmental stress are common. Also, I believe that the impact of climate change can be divided into two distinct drivers of migration:

Climate processes driver , such as sea-level rise, shortage of agricultural land, desertification and growing water scarcity and climate events , such as flooding, storms. But, non-climate drivers, such as government policy, population growth and community level resilience to natural disaster are also important. All contribute to the degree of people's adaptive level.

The climate change problem is one of time (the speed of change) and scale (the number of people it will affect). Although, temporary migration is as an adaptive response to climate stress is already apparent in many areas. But the ability to migrate is a function of mobility and resources (both financial and social). IN other words, the people most to climate change are not necessary the one's most likely to migrate among of different migration factors. In fact, predicting future flows of climate migrants is complex. Professor Myers' estimate of 200 million climate migrants by 2050 year has become the accepted figure-cities in respected publications from the IPCC to the Stern Review on the economics of climate change (Stern, N., Ed. 2006).Hence, it seems that there will have many different factors to cause climate migrant number rising in the future.

Consequently, migration and resettlement may be the most threatening short-term effects of climate change on human settlements. People may decide to migrate in any of the following cases. They includes: loss of housing (because of river, or sea flooding or mudslides), loss of living resources (like water, energy and food supply or employment affected by climate changes); loss of social and cultural resources (loss of cultural properties, neighborhood or community networks).

The three main climate change impacts to influence people to live may include that sea level rise: rising average sea level, sale water intrusion in aquifers, water availability (increase/decrease), extreme weather event: drought, heat waves, violent storms, floods. Thus, if any one of these environment change factors impacts to influence general people's life adaptive level to live anywhere in their any geographic location of their countries. Then, it is possible to influence them to choose to be environmental migrants. It means persons or group of persons who, for compelling reasons of sudden or progressive changes in the environment that adversely affect their lives or living conditions are obliged to leave their habitual homes, or choose to do so, either temporarily or permanently and who move either within their country or abroad. Thus, climate change can let them to feel that it is one unsafe natural disaster and it only brings negative effect to them when they still choose to live in their home town. It refers to situations where people are displaced across boarders in the context of sudden or slow onset disasters or in the context of the adverse effects of climate change.

In forces to non-forces mobility psychological view point, environmental refugee will have these three stages to decide migration: First stage is , refugee –like situation stage, it is very low level control over the whole process , vulnerability. Second stage is, environmentally driven displacement stage, it is compelled, but voluntary, more control over timing and direction and less vulnerability than refugees, but less control and more vulnerability than migrants. Final stage is migrant like situations stage, it is greater control over the process and less vulnerability , even if people are moving in response to deteriorating conditions (Hugo, G. 1996).

Consequently, climate change will be one main important factor to cause any country people who choose to do environmental migrants decision to compare other factors. IT seems, that climate change factor and environment migrant which have close relationship to cause any country people who choose to migrate more than social , economy , less crime, education, cultural , job change, standard of life etc. different external non-natural environment factors.

Reference

Hugo, G. (199). Environmental concerns and International migration. International migration Review., 30. Pp. 105-131.

Mendelsohn , R., (2013) " Climate Change And Economic Growth Commission On Growth And Development" working paper no 60.

Stern, N., (ed.) The economics of climate change: The Stern Review, Cambridge University Press, Cambridge, 2006, p.3.

Stern, N. (2007). The Economics Of Climate Change: The Stern Review, Cambridge UK: University Press.

UNHCR/WFP (United Nations High Commission For Refugees) World Food Program, 2009. Acute Malnutrition in protected refugee situation: A global strategy Geneva: UNHCR/WFP.

Zarocostas , J. 2011. Famine and disease threaten millions in drought hit horn of Africa. BMJ 343: doi: 10,1136/ bmj.d4a4a <online 21 July 2011>.

Climate change how influences global energy need ?

We are facing global warmth and natural resource and energy shortage challenges. Due to our Earth have limited natural resource numbers to supply to us to manufacture energy, but global population has been increasing every year. Thus, it is possible that we have energy shortage crisis. Also, manufactures are spending too much energy to waste to manufacture any products, the energy will cause air or water pollution in manufacturing process or drivers are driving their vehicles to pollute air on the roads. Then it will cause global warmth crisis. How we can avoid these both crises to occur. I shall give some recommendation as below:

Primary energy exploration method

- Greenhouse primary gas energy

Have you ever seen a greenhouse? A greenhouse can trap heat in the sunlight and keeps the air inside the greenhouse warm enough for plants to grow. The glass roof and walls of a greenhouse let in sunlight but prevent heat from escape, this makes the greenhouse warm inside. Similarly, some gases in the Earth's atmosphere can trap heat from the sun and keep the Earth warm. This is called the greenhouse effect. The gases energy that can trap heat from the sun are called greenhouse gases. It is future one kind of potential primary energy to reduce environmental pollution new energy products for human consuming.

- Underwater primary water energy

The world's underwater meeting took place around a table about five meters underwater. Many scientists believe that due to melting of ice caused by global warming, the sea level will rise by as much as 1 m by the end of this century. If the level of the sea rises in the future, most regions of the country will be underwater.

Questions
What impact of global warming is mentioned by underground water?
Can human apply underwater water technology to explore natural underground water energy to avoid global warming threat?

Why do we need to Safety in using fuel and handle gas leaks? Why do we feel town gas smell? How is electricity located at electric station far away from town area? How to solve problems caused by the use of fossil fuels? How to reduce the use of fossil fuels?
To solve the problems, the best way is to reduce our used of fossil fuel. This helps prevent fossil fuels form being used up too quickly. Also, it helps us to reduce environmental problems because fewer pollutants are given out when less fossil fuels are used. Can human help to reduce the use of fossil fuels? Fossil fuels are mainly in power station. Although we use some fossil fuels for our gas cooker and car, it won't make much difference if I use less.

Fossil fuel is not used renew primary energy. Most of energy we use come from fossil fuels, for example, the electricity we use is generated in power stations by burning fossil fuels. The buses we ride use diesel oil. Therefore, we can help reduce the use of fossil fuels by saving energy in our daily lives.

The actions that we can take such as: setting the air-conditioner to a higher temperature, walking instead of using lift, taking a short shower instead of a bath. This reduces the use of the hot water and thus the energy needed to heat the water. Thus, many people can help a lot to reduce our use of fossil fuels to avoid fossil fuel shortage risk occurrence.

For Hong Kong people energy consumption case, how much energy is used when a person travels from Hong Kong to Beijing by airplane? (The distance between Hong Kong and Beijing is about 2000 km). How much energy is used when Hong Kong people take a bus form Tai PO city to Central city? How much energy is used if Hong Kong people drive a car instead? (The driving distance between Tai Po city and Central city is 10Km).

Science explorer, we can visit the England website. Find ways to reduce energy usage from UK people energy using methods. Energy is very important to us. We need energy to walk and carry on any actions. We need energy to grow. We also need energy from food to survive. Without energy, we will die. All machines we use need energy. Without energy the electrical appliances in our homes won't work, the machines in factories will stop.

There are different forms of energy, e.g. light, heat, sound, wind, water, electrical kinetic, chemical and potential energy. Some form energy is primary energy and it can not renew to use, e.g. light, sound, wind, water, fossil fuel etc. Some form energy is secondary energy and it can renew to use in possible, e.g. nuclear, electric charge battery etc. Why does human need to concern how to manufacture secondary energy? Because it is possible that our natural resource will be consumed all, thus we will face primary energy shortage risk. If human can invent any new form of man-made secondary energy to renew to use in order to avoid primary energy shortage to supply to use to use, then human won't only depend on our Earth natural resource energy supply numbers. We can invent any new secondary energy to renew to use again either replaces primary energy or instead of primary energy limit number supply.

What is energy change? For television energy change power case. Firstly, electrical energy changes to television power to be used by television itself, then it changes to light power, next it changes to light power. How to choose fuel form to use? Due to energy can change to different form of powers to supply different form of power advantages to supply to human to use, so it is possible that we can also invent any secondary man made renew used energy to change different form powers to supply us to use, e.g. nuclear energy changes to light or sound or heat form of powers ; electrical charge batteries changes to light or sound or heat form powers to satisfy our daily life needs.

For primary natural resource fuel energy example, different fuel has different feature, e.g. easy to burn, safe to use, gives out a lot of energy, inexpensive, produces little air pollution, easy to transport and store. How can we use in different channels, such as heating food, hot pat, driving vehicles.

For example, although coal is not expensive to cause electricity energy for past transportation tool, e.g. traditional coal energy train or our daily home cooking, but it has negative influence to environment air pollution. Hence, we ought to follow the primary natural resource energy's feature to decide how to apply what aspects of our life needs.

For example, if the country's people hope to reduce pollution when who use any kind of energy, e.g. US , Europe energy markets. The energy entrepreneur ought concentrate on manufacturing the kind of energy which can reduce environment pollution to be the least level to supply the country people to use, e.g. electric charge battery supplies to these countries' drivers to drive their vehicles on the roads, wind energy or water energy to manufacture electricity power supply to reduce air or water pollution ; or if the country people hope to buy the inexpensive energy to use, even the energy's quality and performance is worse, e.g. China, India, Hong Kong markets. The energy entrepreneur ought concentrate on manufacturing the lowest cost and enough supply of natural resource to manufacture the kind of energy to sell cheap price to these countries to use, e.g. China, Africa can accept to use e.g. gas, coal, fuel energy to use to compare developed countries people, e.g. UK, US; or if the countries people who hope to use energy which can easy to transport and store, e.g. light coal. The energy entrepreneur can choose to concentrate on manufacturing much coal to supply to the countries people to use, e.g. China, Arica Thus, to choose to manufacture which kinds of energy supply to the countries market people to use, the energy entrepreneur how decides to manufacture which kind of energy, it depends on which kinds of fuel advantages of the countries people most concerning.

How climate change influences migrant decision to bring economy

influence ? How and why climate change influence migrant right change ? When migrant right change, how it influence migrant immigrating desire ? The interlinkages between climate change and human rights are deep and complex, with climate change impacting a wide range of internationally protected human rights; such as rights to health and even life and rights to food, water, shelter and property. In this paper, I am going to discuss the effect of climate change on protected human rights relating to migration, focusing primarily on the relationship between international refugee law and climate change.

There remains uncertainty on how severe global warming

will be and its precise impacts on society, but there is a 97 per cent consensus among experts that a rapid build-up of greenhouse gas is due to human activities.The Earth's climate is gradually changing due to the continuous concentration of anthropogenic greenhouse gas (GHG) emissions into the atmosphere. The Earth's surface temperature is getting warmer at a disturbing rate, and has become significantly warmer in the last 150 years after 10,000 years of relative stability.[3] Most climate change projections are based on a two-degree Celsius increase in global mean temperature from the temperature in 1850, which has now been agreed by most States as the threshold for 'dangerous' climate change.

The consequences of climate change are more obvious now due to the increased prevalence of rising sea levels, extreme weather conditions, drought and desertification, and these consequences will have significant effects on the ecosystem, specifically on food security, migration, and health. The political, economic, and social capacity of a country, which includes its infrastructure, economic stability, and ability to help its population when in need, will affect individual's ability to cope with the impacts of climate change, and therefore the impacts will be felt differently in different communities. In the 1980s and 1990s, climate change was primarily viewed as an environmental and scientific issue, but in 1990 the potential impacts of climate change on human migration were identified by the Intergovernmental Panel on Climate Change (IPCC). The IPCC stated that millions of people would likely be uprooted by shoreline erosion, coastal flooding, and agricultural disturbances (such as salination of crops),and that climate change might require consideration of 'migration and resettlement outside of national boundaries.

However, the relationship between climate change and forced migration has emerged as one of the most studied, but contested, fields of inquiry, and the lack of agreement on the links between climate change and forced migration explains why the call for the recognition of so-called 'climate change refugees' has been unsuccessful. Legally, there is no such thing as a 'climate change refugee,' and this point will be expanded upon later in this paper, but there is, however, evidence that people are moving in response to the effects of climate change. Cross-border displacement resulting from natural disasters and the effects of climate change has therefore been identified as a normative gap in the international legal protection regime.Determining how exactly climate change affects people's decisions to move is crucial in determining how appropriate the call for the inclusion of people displaced by gradual or sudden environmental impacts within the refugee protection framework.

As discussed above, there is an ongoing debate and scepticism as to the direct link between climate change and displacement, but there is now mounting evidence which supports the plight of so-called 'climate change refugees' and demands attention from the international legal community. The term 'climate change refugee' is often used to describe those who will be forced to leave their homes because of climate change impacts. In this section, I will focus on the extent to which international refugee law may apply, and discuss why, by and large, it is an inappropriate framework for responding to the needs of the displaced.

The first official use of the term 'climate change refugee' was by Essam El-Hinnawi in a United Nations Environment Programme (UNEP) report, where he described people who are forced to leave their places of residence because of human or naturally induced environmental issues as 'environmental refugees'. El-Hinnawi was not trying to make a legal argument for the extension of refugee law to cover those displaced for environmental reasons, but instead was using the term to highlight the potentially devastating effects of unchecked development and pollution. Since then the term has been used in almost any discussion involving the impacts of climate change and forced migration. While those displaced internally (within their own countries) can be protected using the United Nations Guiding Principles on Internal Displacement mechanism, or even by the national law of their own countries, those displaced by environmental impacts and who are crossing or wish to cross their countries' borders currently have no legal basis for this type of movement in international law.

The relationship between climate change, natural disasters, and migration

What is the positive or negative impacts when climate change causes disasters and then bring migration number increases or decreases? The relationship between climatic shocks, natural disasters, and migration has received increasing attention in recent years and is quite controversial. One view suggests that climate change and its associated natural disasters increase migration. An alternative view suggests that climate change may only have marginal effects on migration. Knowing whether climate change and natural disasters lead to more migration is crucial to better understand the different channels of transmission between climatic shocks and migration and to formulate evidence-based policy recommendations for the efficient management of the consequences of disasters.

What are the positive and negative impacts when climate change causes natural disasters and migration attributes? I shall indicate as below:

On migration benefit aspect, it may include these such as: migration can help people cope with the adverse effects of climatic shocks by providing them with new opportunities and resources. Remittances from overseas migrants increase after disasters in their home countries and play an important role in mitigating the adverse effects of climatic shocks and natural disasters. Climatic factors, such as natural disasters or rainfall and temperature variations, may increase international migration through their effect on internal migration. Agricultural productivity represents one of the pathways that can explain the relationship between climatic shocks and migration.

However, climate change may also bring these disadvantages on migration benefit aspect, they may include such as: Public intervention both before and after disasters helps build resilience and can explain why migration responses differ according to different shocks. The migration response to disasters depends on the nature of the shock (slow vs rapid onset events), its severity, and the vulnerability of the affected people.Due to liquidity constraints, poor people might not be able to migrate in the aftermath of climatic shocks. Also, in developing countries, international migration due to disasters may be driven by highly educated people, which may foster brain drain in a vulnerable context.

Climate Change and the Migrant Crisis

What is climate change and migrant crisis ? It may include as below:

For India example, when climate change , it can influence

India migrant decision. India has the first airport which is solely functioning on solar energy. The world can learn from India or China. The West has to stop dumping subsidized agar products into third world destroying local agar industry and pushing people into poverty. Western fisheries are just taking all fish from coasts of Africa. If these policies continue, europeans dont complain people coming to your countries. For afria example, Africa has tripled their population from 400 million to over 1.2 billion people in the past 40 years. Overpopulation, not climate change is their root problem. Africa now has 1 and quarter billion Africans living in some of the world's wort market places. This new lie (scheme) is a dreamed up scheme to import as many as they can into the first world market places, Europe, u.s., Australia, place them on welfare, make the tax payers foot the bill for all the goods and services they can consume to maximize annualized corporate profits making, and to turn them into citizens and have the tax payers pay to educate them so hopefully they will in the future expand taxes uptake for the government's. All paid for by the tax payers. you get to be absorbed genetically. So, it seems that climate change will bring more negative impact to migrants , when the country can attract many migrants choose to emigrate to the county to live, due to climate change infuences.

● Vulnerable countries number will increase when climate change become worse to influence human live as well as human needs to learn new skills to adapt difficult lives

The relationship between migration and the environment is not new. From the mid-19th century Great Irish Famine to the early 20th century Dust Bowl, we have many examples in history of people choosing or being forced to migrate because of changes in their physical environments. What is new now is that the world is grappling with the devastating impacts of climate change. With greater awareness came increased political recognition and there is now a widespread consensus on the need to address the adverse impacts of climate change on the migration of people now and in the future.

Climate migration is a reality in all parts of the world, however, the situation in what is known as "vulnerable countries" represents a particular challenge. Vulnerable countries are Least Developed Countries (LDCs), Landlocked Developing Countries (LLDCs) and Small Island Developing States (SIDS). In 2016, the 15 countries with the highest vulnerability to natural hazards were LDCs, LLDCs and SIDS. These countries are disproportionately affected by the negative impacts of climate change and are often least able to cope due to their structural constraints and geographical disadvantages. At the same time, they contribute the least to climate change. These countries are among the strongest advocates for more robust action on climate migration as they face very real challenges that affect all aspects of the daily lives of their populations.

Climate migration challenges take multiple forms in these vulnerable countries. In LDCs, the poorest and most vulnerable segment of the international community, climate change pressures can intersect with numerous development-related challenges as well as security issues. The combination of those factors often leads people to migrate in search of better or safer lives. For example, the Lake Chad Basin is currently experiencing grave environmental degradation, in a context where populations face the violence linked to the presence of groups such as Boko Haram. Migration patterns in that region have been reshaped due to these factors. Some LDCs such as Ethiopia and Bangladesh are sometimes saddled with the "double stress" of having to deal with internal climate migration, while also hosting large numbers of refugees from neighboring countries. LLDCs often have scarce water resources, further depleted by the impacts of climate change. This can create pressure on populations to migrate for better access to water. For example, nomadic pastoralists are often pushed to alter their traditional routes and travel further and for longer periods in search of water and land resources. Climate change is also affecting livelihoods, such as in Mongolia where extremely cold winters called dzud deplete nomadic livestock and destroy agriculture opportunities, pushing rural populations to migrate to urban centers.

SIDS are recognized as a special case for sustainable development as they face greater risk of marginalization due to their small size and remoteness. They also have fragile natural environments, and natural disasters such as storms and cyclones have a devastating impact on the population. The adverse impacts of climate change have contributed to the migration of thousands of people in SIDS in the last decade alone. One specific type of migration in this context is the planned relocation of people, where entire communities need to be moved, generally further inland, to escape climate change impacts such as coastal erosion. In Fiji, following Tropical Cyclone Winston in 2016, more than 60 villages were relocated to reduce people's exposure and vulnerability to further risks.

The current situation is clearly preoccupying and addressing the negative impacts of climate change on the migration of people in vulnerable countries should represent a priority now and for the future. We are moving towards a high level week of crucial political dialogues at the United Nations General Assembly in September 2019. In particular, the United Nations Climate Action Summit is a key opportunity to highlight the challenges of most vulnerable countries and put forward commitments and solutions to address climate migration issues.

On conclusion, riority should be given to mitigate the impacts of climate change and promote climate change adaptation in places where populations are at risk of forced migration. However, it is also clear that in some places, it will not be possible for populations to remain in situ and it is of utmost importance to think about how legal migration options can be offered to those migrants. It is also important to factor in the positive role that migrants can play in the fight against climate change, such as by facilitating remittances and transfer of skills and knowledge towards climate action. So, climate change influences human needs to change skills to adapt difficult lives.

How climate change impacts on developing countries economy ?

In fact, climate change will increase global temperature change rainfall patterns and will result in more frequent and severe floods and drought. Depending on future emission of greenhouse gases, global temperatures are likely to rise between 2 degree and 4 degree within the next century. The main impacts of climate change will however not be felt through higher temperatures, but through a change in the hydrological cycle. Rainfall is likely to increase around the poles and the tropics when in the sub-tropics average precipitation is likely to decrease. Not only the average annual or seasonal rainfall will change, there also be an increase in the number of extreme events resulting in most frequent and severe floods and droughts.

How does climate change influence to development countries? Climate change will influence any development countries on these several aspects. They include as below:

On trade influence hand, reducing emission levels from the developing world is extremely important. If current developments are continuing, for example, emissions from China and India both countries will save be much higher than the total emission form all Europe countries. Currently, the Europe is stimulating mitigation and transfer of clean technologies through the clean development mechanism (CDM). Although, it is still unclear what the mitigation potential of the (CDM) is, especially in India the investment is (CDM) projects is significant. However, the Europe should take a much wider approach. In developing countries a lot can be done in terms of increasing energy efficiency, land use change and agriculture. It is also important that developing countries are stimulated to choose a sustainable, low emission developed pathway. Choices for more sustainable, low emission technologies should be made early in the process. It seems that climate changing will encourage many countries will choose to do more environment protection related trading, e.g. researching how to invent environment protection new products to reduce our earth pollution between European and any developing countries, such as China and India etc.

On focus mitigation efforts in least developed countries on land use change, agriculture development aspect, in the least developed countries mitigation efforts should not focus on the energy or transport sector, but on agriculture and forestry. Agriculture is responsible for a relatively large percentage of the emissions in many developing countries, e.g. Africa, China, Malaysia, Hong Kong, Japan etc. In this sector there are many win options both reducing poverty and reducing greenhouse gas emissions. For example, improved water and nutrient management can sharply increase production efficiency and reduces at least the amount of emission per kg food produced. Agro-forestry reduces greenhouse gas emission through increased carbon storage and reduces poverty through diversifying the incomes of local communities.

However, in most developing countries, the main limitation in coping with the impacts of climate change is a lack of capacity. Besides a lack of capacity, in many developing countries, there is also a significant lack of data and knowledge on climate change impacts. Developing countries should be stimulated to improve data gathering and make existing data more easily available.However, no migration effort will stop the need for adaptation. Especially, the least developed countries, who have contributed little to the problem will suffer the most.

On business strategies for climate change aspect, nowadays, the valuation for clean-technology companies, have increased considerable and the corporate carbon footprint has become an important topic to be discussed how to solve among senior managers? How can firms profit from what they do to address climate change? Thus, a low-carbon economy is already especially in energy, transport and heavy industry.

If current climate science holds true and there is considerable uncertainty in the estimates, global greenhouse gas emissions should ideally decrease from today's levels by 90 percent as of 2050 year in order to certain global warming below two degrees centigrade.

Hence, it seems global warmth challenge brings further any new energy potential development businesses. Due to environment scientists encourage us to be realized the necessary increase in carbon productivity and new low-carbon technologies that are necessary dramatically reduces energy consumption and direct greenhouse gas emissions will have to be developed and then implemented widely to avoid future serious global environment warmth caused climate changes and pollution challenges occurrence.

FOUR

MARKETING STRATEGY HOW INFLUENCES CONSUMER BEHAVIOR

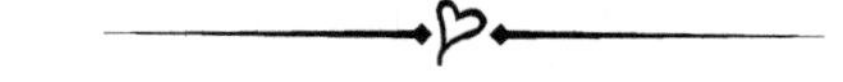

How can Marketing mix strategy solve supermarket store organizational cooperation challenge ?

The place(P) of the traditional marketing mix decides about channel intermediaries or middlemen to use an outdated, yet user friendly, term and the management of physical distribution. Placing products involves managing the process supporting the flow of goods or services from producers to consumers.The process has sometimes been described as developing the best routes to market for a firm's products. Products must be made available in the right quantity, in the right location, and at the times when customers wish to purchase them. Marketing channels can perform an important role in the later stages of a value chain, in particular outbound logistic (e.g. order processing, storage and transportation); marketing and sales (e.g. market research, personal selling, sales promotion) and after sales service. However, it depends on which kinds of business to need outbound logistic, such as Tesco supermarket only needs ordering fresh fruit and vegetables from local farmers, then these foods need to be stored in refrigerate in warehouse and transport these foods to different supermarkets by vans. So, Tesco value chain only needs outbound logistic activity, but it does not need marketing and sales and after sale service to sell its fresh fruit and vegetables to its clients from its supermarkets (stores). In fact, Tesco stores is such UK farmer's intermediaries which can add value by breaking bulk. This might involve purchasing in large quantities of fruits and vegetables from UK local farmers and then selling smaller, more manageable, to keep volumes of fresh food stock in warehouses, then its vans will deliver these fresh fruits and vegetables to different stores daily. Discrepancies of fruit foods quantity are reduced by Tesco (intermediary) who provides every store clients with individual preferable fresh foods items that suit their needs daily. Tesco stores can offer superior knowledge of a target market compared with farmers, for example by ensuring which kinds of vegetables or fruits foods numbers are stocked in every store to match the economic and lifestyle needs of Tesco store shoppers who live in the area. Probably the most important gaps between Tesco store shoppers and UK local farmers in channel management are indicated at those of location and time. A location gap occurs owing to the geographic separation of farmers and the store shoppers of their fresh fruit and vegetables foods. UK farmers generally want to grow their fruits and vegetable food in one central location (farming), but farmers' food buyers typically want to buy their growing foods locally. A time gap arises when the UK local farmers' fresh foods buyers want to buy whose fresh growing foods at a time when a UK local farmer may considerate it inconvenient to make the available. UK local farmers may like to grow fresh fruits and vegetable foods at night from 8:00 PM to 12:00PM, then who will collect these fresh foods from 5:00 AM to 7:00 in the morning, but their buyers may want to buy in the evenings or at weekends afternoon. Tesco stores (intermediary) need to facilitate vans to transport these fresh fruits and vegetables foods from farmers' farming to its one central warehouse to deliver to different stores to sell the budget numbers of different kinds of foods to every local store consumers more exactly (Adrian, P. 2012).

Tesco stores is one of the world's largest retailers, it has social responsibility to protect fresh fruit and vegetable to sell to clients. It had attempted to predict customer behavior about hope much fresh fruit and vegetable and what kinds of fresh fruit and vegetable whose consumers will buy from data statistic in warehouse. It aims to reduce excess fruit and vegetable stocks in warehouse to cause perishable. In the winter might have seen choice reduced to basic items such as potatoes, cabbage, apples, supplemented by canned fruit and vegetables. Look in a Tesco supermarket today, and clients may find difficult to tell the season of the year or the distance from the countryside, simple based on the fruit and vegetables with are on display. In UK supermarket sector is intensely competitive, and has seen continuous innovation in the way it seeks to satisfy customers' needs. As consumers have become wealthier, the supermarkets realized that buyers would no longer be content with the staple foods such as cabbage and potatoes in the depths of winter-significant numbers of them now wanted excitement on a plate, and all year round. Furthermore, if they were planning a menu, they wanted to be sure that when they went to their local supermarket.

By and large, supermarkets have been key drivers of the value for the groceries that they sell. They have been close to their customers and identified their changing needs. They have built confidence with their customers, who can trust freshness and provenance of food they sell and the reliability of supply. It is therefore the supermarkets who have gone seeking sources of supply, rather than growers aggressively seeking to sell the produce that they have available. Before, the development of very large supermarket chains, retailers were more fragmented. They did not have the power or resources to innovate with new product lines which they could then commission a grower to produce. Today, supermarket such as Tesco invest heavily in their food technology laboratories, and can then go to suppliers and place large orders with exacting standards with regard to price, quality, and delivery. Above all else, supermarkets have put themselves at the center of a slick distribution system which connects an international networks of growers through transport networks of trucks, ships and planes to put fresh produce in their network of stores, every day, all year around. The efficiency of the logistics, and the bargaining power of the supermarkets has often led to the price being charged at a British supermarket being lower than the price changed in supermarkets thousands of miles away where fruit and vegetables were grown. Tomatoes grown in Bulgaria and sold in Britain can be cheaper in Britain in local Bulgarian shops. The bizarre situation has occurred where the supermarkets import apples from France to be sold in Kent, the traditional home of British apple growing, plums from Poland to be sold in the grown product in Lincolnshire. Supermarkets argue that sourcing from overseas is not just an issue of cost saving more importantly, the supermarkets seek a continuity of supplies from large growers who can guarantee to deliver a specified quantity at a specified quantity at a specified time and place. The supermarkets capable of achieving this. British supermarkets are among the most efficient in the world, and their desire to ensure that customers can always get what they want may explain the mass transport of food. Local farmers' market may could environmentally friendly, but they rarely guarantee a continuity of supplies. As part of their drive for efficiency, supermarkets have a tendency to move food , such potatoes could being transported several hundred miles between distribution centers before they end up on a supermarket shelf just a few miles from where potatoes were grown. The environmental campaigning group Sustain has estimated that the average children travels 2,000 between the farm where it was grown and the supermarket shelf and furthermore the distance products travel from farm to end customer increased by an estimated 25 per cent between 1980 year and 2007 year (Priesnitz 2007).

Global warming had become an important issue with many clients and there was growing concern that supermarkets' practice of transporting fresh produce long distances around the world was irresponsibly adding to greenhouse gas emissions. Hence, distance travelled was one of value chain factor Terso supermarket needs to consider their fruit and vegetables food to keep fresh in refrigerate to transport to retailers to sell in UK. The most contentious food miles are clocked up by fresh fruit and vegetables flow in by plane from overseas. Although, air freighted produce accounted for less than 1 per cent of total UK food miles, it was the fastest growing way of moving foods around. One response By Tesco was to introduce a greatest proportion of local produce. To achieve this, it placed buyers and marketing teams in the regions in order to get a clear picture of local markets and to develop relationships with suppliers. By 2007 year, Tesco claimed to have 7,000 regional lines from throughout the UK, which were promoted as local produce, supporting local growers and reducing greenhouse gas emissions. Throughout its history, Tesco has demonstrated its ability to listen to what customers want, and this has been true in respect of its distribution system. The weaknesses of commodity systems are particularly for major customers, such as Mc Donalds, commodity systems do not lead to reliability in supply, quality, quantity or price nor high rates of innovation on which they can differentiate their offer from their competitors. The opportunity and challenge of fresh food product differentiation, so Tesco stores need to innovation to give rise to a number of strategic options to keep vegetables and fruits to be fresh in the short time to sell full numbers. If a firm, such as Tesco is the lowest cost producer than commodity market strategy can be an attractive strategic option. As Tesco stores fresh food sale that it's larger competitors shall find difficult to copy. Otherwise, Smaller size stores can sometimes be a competitive advantage.

Tesco stores (fresh food retailer) need to co-operate with suppliers and fresh food growers to align the whole chain to the changing needs of consumers. The food chain strategy aims to deliver superior value to specific groups of customers. Tesco stores work closely with its fresh food suppliers to develop specific products for each range. Both the supplier and growers understand the Tesco marketing strategy and their role in the innovation process. Tesco is actively seeking new chain ideas and is prepared to pay for such efforts. From a primary producer and supplier perspective the range of brands enables Tesco to work with suppliers to market the total crop .

How and why can global human innovation factor influence China culture and product need change ?
How innovation is influenced to the Chinese economy by global competitive environment? Does China have the innovative capacity to raise any kinds of the number of technological product productivity, create more high value-added technological jobs and achieve its global technological export market aspirations? Whether global competitive technological changing environment will bring positive or negative impact to influence China technological product export and import market?

To answer above these questions? I shall assume that however, if China expected its any kinds of technological products can be innovated to manufacture to sell to foreign (overseas) markets successfully. China's any technological product companies need to consider how to mix in global technological product sale market environment. In the global competitive technological product industry, where innovation requires original inventions or engineering breakthroughs, such as branded pharmaceuticals and automatic vehicles. China has small shares of global technological product market, but in any technological product industry, where innovation is about meeting unmet consumer needs or driving efficiencies in technological manufacturing, appliances and solar panels etc. these future innovative technological products for example. It is one kind of technological innovative products in the future. However, China's massive consumer market and unmatched manufacturing ecosystem give it unique advantages in these sectors, perhaps the most popular e-commerce and consumer electronic companies in China, such as Alibaba and Xiaomi are rapidly as to global players.

In fact, China has made the necessary investments in research and development and education to improve its performance in science and engineering based industries. The major successfully China's technological includes high speed rail and telecommunications equipment prove that under the right investment. Chinese technological companies can be one major technological product exporter among global competitors in engineering based industries. And even now, in science-based industries, such as biopharmaceuticals, Chinese companies has fast speed of some technological product manufacturing market to become more stronger innovators.

Consequently, global innovation factor encourages market based competitors within more China technological industry and make China more attractive to top science talent, it seems that China can succeed in all forms of innovation. Also, time factor will be critical to influence China's any technological product qualities and productivities . China is facing slowing GDP growth, and aging increasing population and declining returns on massive fixed investment. China must find ways to raise productivity. Innovation will be the major key to this sustainable growth path in the long future time.

Finally, why can innovative factor be important to influence China's technological product manufacturing of quality and productivity? Given these trends, I shall indicate the reasons as below:

Firstly, innovation means to attempt to catch up with advanced economies by absorbing and adapting technologic al , best practices and technological knowledge from overseas. Thus, I suggest Chinese companies can invest technology to foreign directly, purchases of equipment and joint ventures (cooperation) with overseas companies to do any technological research or invention or manufacturing any technological products together. As a result, China now ranks second in the world in knowledge intensive flows movement of knowledge intensive any technological products or services and foreign direct technological investment successfully (OECD, McKinsey Global Institute Analysis).

Secondly, within these foreign technological organizations, specific technical committees are established to develop standards for a given technology or area of interest. Within technical committees, working groups of experts propose, test, debate and adopt protocols to incorporate into the final standard. Inclusion of technologies or approval of protocols accomplished through consensus and majority vote.

Thirdly, the formal technological standardization organizations in China have developed over the past technology year under the influence of the 1989 year. Technology standardization law rapidly changed technologies, and high degrees of experimentation and learning. In particular reform proper role for intellectual property, both foreign and domestic in technology standards. Critically, however, the reforms do not challenge

, the centrality of the state is the initiator and approver of technology standard.

In conclusion, in the global technological competitive changing environment influence, it brings positive and negative impacts to influence China technological product development. On the positive impact hand, it encourages China needs to innovate its technology to keep its competitive effort to export technological products to foreign market. On the negative impact hand, it raises the technological competition to China. Consequently, globalization brings technological innovation to global technological business market, but it also damage global job opportunities to the low knowledge and technician workers to cause their unemployment, due to high technological worker needs will be risen in the future.

Case study change in the marketing environment on sales of ready meals to supermarket, such as Walt Mark strategy ?

Using an appropriate framework of analysis, briefly summarize the effects of change in the marketing environment on sales of ready meals. Although, previously dismissed and a poor substitute for real cooking and ready meal sales have grown rapidly in recent years in many western developed countries, such as UK, France or Germany. But, Ready meal manufacturers ready to respond to a changing marketing environment. Due to one big change in recent year has been growing demand for ready prepared meals bought from a supermarket. An analysis of the reasons for the growth in the ready prepared meals markets indicates the effects of boards factors in the marketing environment on the size of a particular market. In fact, this food market is changing to drive the growth in the ready meals market, but there are differences in the food market potential between countries. The effect of change in the marketing environment on sales of ready meals, such as technology has played a big role in the growing take up of ready meals and new technologies have allowed companies to develop ready meals which preserve taste and texture, which still making them easy to use by the consumer.

Furthermore, great advances in distribution management, in particular the use of information technology to control inventories, has allowed fresh, chilled ready meals to be effectively and efficiently distributed without the need for freezing or added preservatives. Ready meals particularly appeal to single householders, which individual family members tend to eat at different times, so family meals together remains stronger in many continental European countries than in the UK individual ready meals. Young people have lost the ability to cook creatively, as cookery has been reduced in importance in the school, so young clients group will rise to buy ready meals from supermarket. Marketing can be seen as a system that must respond to environmental change. A food market can be defined as a meeting place for stakeholder (consumers) and sellers. Food market can be set up in a supermarket or restaurants. A food market consists of the individual's target taste, such as older group, family group, young group or business clients who are actual or potential caters of a restaurant meals or supermarket package of foods. Grocery stores (supermarkets) have an influence of meals (fast cooked food) outlets in low income urban areas, which has contributed to the income in access to healthy foods. An organization's marketing environment means the individuals, organizations, and forces external to the marketing management's ability to develop and maintain successful exchanges with its customers. The marketing environment to ready meal manufacturers had three levels.

Firstly, it includes the micro environment, it describes those elements that impinge directly on the ready meal manufacturers themselves, so the micro environment of ready meal manufacturers which include business clients who have direct contact, such as restaurants, supermarkets and individual clients who have direct contact. Otherwise, supermarket shoppers, restaurant clients and food supply competitors who have no direct contract to ready meal manufacturers, so who won't include in food market micro environment to ready meal manufacturers. Secondly, it includes the macro environment, it describes things that are beyond the immediate environment but can nevertheless affect an organization, so the macro environment of ready meal manufacturers which include the export countries' economies forces, such as unemployment ratio, GDP; technological forces, such as the export countries' factories food productive technology; social/ cultural forces, such as the export countries' people taste acceptance; political/legal forces, such as the export countries' import food quota numbers. Thirdly, it includes the internal environment, it describes ready meal manufacturers' employees and equipment and finance and functional responsibilities.

Environment means everything outside influences the person, in contrast with individual or personal variables . The effects of change in the marketing environment on sales of ready meals can be analyzed by creating healthy food and eating environment changing factor and supermarket technological changing factor as below:

The ready meal manufacturers could not ignore threats to the natural ecological environment change Due to the food companies could have technology to manufacture good taste cooked ready meals to provide to supermarkets to sell. Thus, it might influence the consumers to decide whether restaurants or supermarkets or ready meals suppliers who could provide the most reasonable price and taste to satisfy whose eating needs every day. Thus, it caused the growing demand for ready prepared cooked meals bought from supermarkets. Due to it was possible that consumers felt to eat ready cooked meals in expensive restaurants or who did not like to buy foods to cook from food suppliers or who could not feel which could supply more good food taste and health food quality to compare supermarkets specially. Otherwise, although, supermarkets could provide cheaper ready cooked meals to satisfy who to feel good food taste and health food quality. Due to ready meal manufacturers had new techniques to develop ready meals which preserve taste and texture, which still making them easy to use to eat by the consumers.

Furthermore, great advances in distribution management, in particular the use of information technology to control inventories, has allowed fresh , chilled ready meals to be effectively and efficiently distributed to supermarkets or restaurants without the need for freezing or added preservatives. Creating healthy food and eating environments view describes an ecological framework for conceptualizing the many food environments and conditions that influence food choices, with an emphasis on current knowledge was been regarding the home, child care, school, work site, retail store and restaurant settings. The status of measurement and evaluation of nutrition environment and the need of action to improve health are highlighted in marketing environment. More processed and convenience foods are available in large portion sizes and which were supplied at relatively low prices at supermarkets. Parents are working larger hours, there are fewer family meals and more meals are eaten away from home. The school food environment is remarkably different. It seemed that it would be changed in the marketing environment on sales of ready cooked meals to supermarket more easily. Due to supermarkets' cooked meals should focus on selling high calorie and low nutrition foods are available in multiple venues throughout the school student client group target because it was possible that supermarkets could sell ready cooked ready meals prices were more cheaper to compare to restaurants or school canters' cooked meals provided prices.

The effects of change in the marketing environment on sales of ready meals which indicated that consumers chose prefer to buy ready cooked meals from supermarkets. It seemed that a restaurant market failure could be caused to arise. For example, there was poor information on the part of food (ready cooked meals) to provide to the restaurant about the foods that consumers in a location(place) would demand for a given price to compare to the supermarket sale prices. The restaurant would lose clients if which cooked the kind of meals to sell higher price to compare to the supermarket sale of the kind of cooked ready meals price possibly. Large size supermarkets could sell cheaper ready cooked meals to low income group clients. It could cause competition to constitute a market failure to small size supermarkets. If the small size supermarkets lacked good information on the true food (ready cooked meals) with concentrations to sell cheaper prices, then this ready cooked meal market failure was one potential reason why small size supermarkets did not locate to close to the large supermarkets. Due to supermarkets grew in size would influence clients' choice to buy the numbers of cooked foods (ready meals) products. Moreover, The advent of computerized logistics and inventory systems were integrated with the large size supermarkets themselves occurred between the 1980 years and 1990 years .

So large size supermarkets were reliance on their own distribution and cooked food (ready meals) inventory systems along with larger supermarket sizes to allow super center to change to sell ready cooked meals at lower prices. Supermarkets marketing can promote healthful eating by increasing availability, affordability or restricting / de-marketing unhealthy foods to sell cooked Food (ready meals) marketing strategy at supermarkets, including labelling, packaging, pricing and point of sale advertising. Consumers' cost saving efforts and income and ready cooked meals prices increasing or decreasing factors can drive the choice of supermarkets as well as cooked meal products use of coupons and loyalty cards bargain shopping is another factor to influence their choice. Private label or store (supermarket) brands are taking an increasing share of consumers shopping dollars as the importance of brands. Supermarket shoppers stated priorities are cooked food (ready meals) quality or taste and price and healthy cooked food (ready meals) choices.

However, supermarket shoppers' buying behaviors don't always reflect on favor healthful foods. Due to demand for locally grown cooked food is increasing. Anyway, restaurant meals are changed to supermarket to sell, which decide what kinds of meals to stock and how many of different kinds of meals to stock and how much variety of kinds of meals to offer to any one supermarket as well as supermarket shoppers prefer fewer options, provided that their preferred brand or cooked food (ready meals) products are available. The designs of supermarket ready cooked meal products and packaging to supermarket to sell is the focus of unusual colors or shape which can be used to increase interest and is specially pervasive among fun foods to compare to restaurant meals. Package design, including where text and images are placed, which can influences cooked foods (supermarket ready meals repurchasing again).The influence of design differs by the type of display consumer segments seek (convenience, information or images) and ready cooked meals package sizes have a relatively strong influence on consumption; larger ready cooked meals packages might increase per-use consumption ,but smaller packages might not improve self regulation and might not actually increase total consumption.

In conclusion, I suggest that this ready meal manufacturers need to give more attention to be paid to food sellers, such as supermarkets' competitive differentiation and understanding the way in which customers attribute value to its ready meal products choice. Moreover, many consumers have become increasingly concerned about the health implication of the food they eat, so ready meal manufacturers will need to continue responding to such concerns. For example, who have responded with a range of low calorie meals, and addressed specific, sometimes transient, health fads, with respect to trans-fatty acids and omega 3 supplements of these cooked meal ingredients. Many consumers have also become concerned about the ecological environment and some supermarket suppliers, such as Marks and Spencer have incorporated sustainability agendas into their ready meals, for example by reducing packaging and sourcing supplies from sustainable sources. Thus, it caused ready meal manufacturers why who needed to give more attention to concern how supermarkets helped them to sell cooked ready meals in this foods market.

Critically discuss the link between the economic environment and sales of ready meals in supermarket. The macro environment, it describes things that are beyond the immediate environment but can nevertheless affect the organization. Such as the ready meal manufacturers in its macro environment, including the economic environment which can cause the manufacturers sell ready meal numbers whether which can sell more or less to different exported countries due to the exported countries' unemployment ratios, GDP and Government policies etc factors influence. Economic theory can help to explain why it can influence consumer behavior. In food sale market, it can include consumer behavior and demand side as well as retailer behavior and supply side two issues.

Consumer behavior and demand side issue, such as the exported countries' consumer whose knowledge of the nutritional benefits of foods whether which prices were raised to choose to buy reasonably as well as retailer behavior and supply side issues, such as investing for developing a restaurant or supermarket in an underserved area whether the types of meals choices which are valued or which are not valued to buy to offer to clients from imports. On the other hand, economic environment factor, individual income can influence who chooses the type, quantity and quality of food that is purchased for a house holder and it also influenced the cooking and storage facilities available in a household to influence food choice.

On the other way, economic environment variation factor can also influence food access across areas. It is important to understand the economic conditions that may contribute to food deserts, that is the costs that food retail businesses face and the choice available to consumers who want to buy foods. Economic environment factor considers the consumer and demand factors, business and supply factors and the market conditions that interact to create differences in the food retail environment across areas and subpopulations. In general, high income meal client group can accept to choose to go to supermarkets or restaurants to spend than low income meal client group. The impact of the economic environment on sales of ready meals is such as an individual get richer, who can afford to buy ready prepared foods, rather than spend time and effort to prepare to cook them at home. It seemed that low income consumers were decreasing to eat meals at expensive restaurant to the alternative of relatively cheap ready prepared meals at home. Research could also consider how consumer knowledge and preferences and the time cost tradeoffs affect consumer decisions of which foods to eat and whether to make or to buy prepared foods from supermarkets or to eat at restaurant meals . Travel costs and time costs of acquiring foods as well as the time costs of preparing foods (meals) are also likely to affect demand for particular foods. Research on price variation at the local level and demand models could also be used to help determine which factors contribute to differences in access to food retailers. Price is also major determinant of food (meal) demand.

The higher, the price of a food(meal), the lower the meal quantity demanded. On the other hand, the higher the price of a substitute food (meal), the higher demand will be for that food (meal) item. Given the budget constraints of low income consumers and the price of some specific foods (meals), low income consumers may substitute higher priced foods (meals) with lower priced foods(e.g. hamburger for steak or canned fruits for fresh fruits). Considering restaurants foods purchasing choice, such as economies of scale, which is when the costs of operating a restaurant decreases as restaurant size increases and economies of scope, which is when the costs decrease as more meals variety increases, suggests that larger restaurants that offer greater variety can offer lower meal prices. Both factors may account for the ability of larger restaurants to survive more easily than smaller restaurants. Considering supermarkets foods purchasing choice, it is possible that food retailers (supermarkets) actually have some market power, especially in setting where there are few competitors to close. It would have an incentive to increase food (ready meal) price and restrict foods(ready meals) supply quantities to increase profit. Supply side conditions, such as economies of scale, it could lead to (ready meal) food retailers (supermarkets) to have more market power, if it was not close between supermarkets. Individual behavior to make healthy choices can occur only in a supportive economic environment with accessible and affordable healthy food choices. Hence, food environment and sale strategies is needed to consider to adopt the exported countries' economic change.

Food marketing client target groups can include home parents, students and working people groups mainly and marketing and economic environment factors would cause food choices and these factors impact health and nutrition and the focus on the connections between people and their environments.

In conclusion, macro level economic environmental factors play a more indirect role but have a substantial and powerful effect on what people eat. Macro level factors operate within the larger society, include food marketing, social norms, food production and distribution systems, agriculture policies and economic price structures as well as social environmental to influence within the home, such as model of healthful dietary intake by parents feeding style, frequent family meals may promote healthful food consumption among children.

Does Ryanair airline need to concern ecological environment protection strategy ?

In recent years, social, economic and environment pressures have pushed airlines to accept their social responsibility. Closely tied to this acceptance is a corporate policy that aims at raising social and environmental standards on a voluntary basis and that means beyond legal and contractual requirement. It means that corporate social responsibility is not just an optional
consideration to core airline business activities, such as airlines industry fuel consumption pollutes sky air to cause global warming problem. Rather, Ryanair airline needs to concern social responsibility because it's fuel emissions would cause negative influence to stakeholders. e.g. causing bad negative climate to influence farmers to grow rice and vegetables etc foods successfully, so global warming will make farmers stakeholder can not earn more income and food buyers stakeholder won't eat rice and vegetables etc. foods easily, even global warming will damage natural environment to cause strong wind or strong raining or water natural hazard to damage any countries' houses to make house owners stakeholder who lose their houses to live.

Hence, in the long term, if Ryanair airline still continue consume too much fuels to use to fly to cause emissions to pollute air to any countries as well as other airlines do not achieve any actions to reduce to consume to use more fuels together efficiently. I believe that global warming will become very serious to influence human living and eating problem occurrence in our earth as soon as possibly. Hence, such as Ryanair airline is among of global airlines, which have responsibility to consider how to reduce fuel consumption to cause too much emissions to pollute air in our earth. Such as, I was Ryanair airline marketing manager , I ought need to let Ryanair airline to measure whether it ought only concern how to sell cheaper air fares and buy many airplanes and consume much fuels to fly to raise income or it ought concern it's fuel emissions to pollute environment to cause global warming to influence global human stakeholders encounter living and eating problem to face natural foods resource shortage to supply in the future.

The ecological concerns global warming problem is serious nowadays, it brings the possible long term harmful consequences of executive emissions to the atmosphere. The developed countries, such as Northern Europe and United States people needed often to play travel entertainment by airlines transportation choice. However, scientists proved airlines used fossil fuels to harm excessive emissions to natural environment which would cause global warming problem to cause devastation of low lying areas to influence natural environment danger, even the developing countries people life and their houses would also encountered to be hazarded in the long term. If I was the marketing manager of an airline, such as Ryanair, I must concern socially responsible needs to Ryanair airline.

Although, Ryanair aircraft had become more efficient in use of fuel during 1990 years, but Ryanair airline's passengers were booming demand to cause to increase aeroplane numbers to supply to satisfy passengers' travel needs and to pursue raising profit aim every year.

In fact, Ryanair airline used fuels to give energy to push aeroplanes to fly and it also polluted sky air during it's aeroplanes often were flying to cause global warming. For example, Ryanair airline marketing strategy was low fare prices to attract to increase many passengers to choose to attract to increase many passengers to choose to sit it's aeroplanes and it designed a cheap weekend break by Mediterranean travel to increase the unknown and remote possibilities of global warming. Hence, Ryanair would increased many new airplanes to increase to use fossil fuels of excessive emissions to the atmosphere to cause the effects of aid rain, poor climate change , destructive winds, rising sea levels and devastation of low lying areas by global warming bad consequences. Hence, it seemed that Ryanair airline had responsibility to concern how to protect natural environment due to its airplanes numbers and passengers were increasing to cause to increase to use more fossil fuels to cause the possible long term harmful consequences of excessive emissions to the sky to bring global warming occurrence nowadays. As I was this Ryanair airline marketing manager, I shall recommend Ryanair airline needed to consider this global warming socially responsible issue due to its airplanes spent too much fossil fuels to cause harmful consequences of excessive emissions to the sky. It would bring threats to developing countries people life and houses by global warming, so it concerned only how to raise itself interest marketing behavior of performance, but it neglect the serious global warming to cause bad influence to any developing countries people life danger, it was possible that passengers would feel it was not a socially responsible airline company, so it could not build a good image to whom in this airline industry and its further passengers would choose its other competitors (socially responsible airline companies) to substitute its airline service provision.

● Discussion

I should suggest Ryanair airline needed to control fossil fuel numbers to reduce to harm excessive emissions to natural environment seriously and it could spend much expenditure to buy good quality of fossil fuels to active the reduction of too much emissions to damage natural environment aim and it could shorten the sky flying distance to fly to other countries' airports from its airport to aim to attempt to reduce to use much fuel to pollute sky air per day and it could cancel some long flight flying routes and increased short flight flying routes to reduce flight spending hours to attempt to reduce to use fossil fuels to provide every airplanes to fly to pollute sky air every day.

Although, these marketing strategies would be possible to reduce airline income, but it would also attract many further passengers to choose to sit to its airplanes to go to travel if it could build good image to prove it was a socially responsible airline to serve passengers to let them to like to choose to use its flying service to go to travel willingly, even it could lead other airlines to follow it to use its marketing strategic methods to reduce to spend too much fossil fuels to pollute sky air to raise global warming problem seriously together. Hence, if Ryanair airline could attempt to achieve to reduce the fossil fuel numbers to use to airplanes to fly , it was possible that the other airline companies should follow it to do the same behaviors to aim to do social responsible organizations to concern how to reduce the global warming problem to cause to harm to our natural environment seriously for long term in the future.

The case study refers to apparent hypocrisy of clients who may claim to be concerned about the environment, but nevertheless continue to fly what might bring about a narrowing of this gap between what consumers think and what they actually do?

In fact, some apparent hypocrisy of consumers who may claim to be concerned about the global warming harmful natural environment problem due to airline companies, e.g. Easy Jet,

Ryanair etc. western countries' airlines which allowed fossil fuels produced harmful consequences of excessive emissions to atmosphere, but nevertheless continue to fly. However, I might recommend these methods to bring about a narrowing of this gap between what consumers think and what they actually do.

I think to bring a narrowing of this gap between consumers were happy to carry on airplanes to fly and it would not influence them to concern about climate change problem at the same time.

There was certainly a possible that governments would intervene. Such as the UK government and European commission had floated the idea of taxing aviation fuel and brought aircraft emissions within scope of the European emission trading scheme. Thus, if these western countries governments raised to charge aviation fuel taxing, it would possible to threaten any western airlines to shorten any flight routes hours and flight flying distance to fly to destination of the countries' airports from these airline companies' every country's airport, so which would not need to use more fuels for its airplanes to use if it had shorten flight flying routes distance to arrive other countries' airports. Hence, the airlines did not want to pay higher aviation tax to government, so which would attempt to shorten some flight flying routes from long distance to be short distance when their airplanes needed to fly to some other countries' airport to aim to buy less fuel numbers or which would not buy more airplanes

Due to they needed to pay high aviation tax expenditure to their countries governments every year. Thus, it was possible that high fuel tax expenditure would cause airlines to shorten flight routes time. The most important, when some airlines decided to buy less fuels. These airlines might bring about a narrowing of this gap between what consumers think and what they actually do and these airlines were possible to raise their competitive ability, due to which would possible to persuade the concerned environment protective passengers who would choose to buy these airlines air tickets to more than to buy the other airlines' air tickets. Due to some airlines could not reduce to buy more fuel numbers to provide their airplanes to fly and which would increase air pollution to sky seriously, those airlines' spending excessive long hours (time) of every flight flying routes to fly to different countries' airports which would use more fuel to fly to cause air pollution to harm natural environment seriously and which would let these clients to feel unhappy to choose to buy air tickets to sit their airplanes possibly. Hence, different governments raised aviation tax would cause many airlines to reduce to buy too much fuel numbers to use possibly. It seemed that airlines needed have a social responsible duty to concern they needed to buy more fuels if they increased airplanes numbers, then they would raise air pollution to cause global warming problem seriously. Hence, I think passengers would not buy air tickets to fly to travel by airplanes when who would have long days of holidays. Otherwise, who would choose to stay at home or who would choose to go to travel by cruises on water transportation on their holidays. However, in western developed economies, legislation to enforce environmentally sensitive methods of productive is increasing, so airlines might adopt environmentally sensitive flight service processes to gain a competitive advantages. The challenges of using fuels resources in more efficient and less polluting way has achieved research and development, e.g. wind power research, solar panels, heat pumps and carbon capture technology have presented opportunities for airlines to improve the efficiency of fuels and airline marketing to business and individual group passengers.

Legal actions to place control over the emission of air pollutants have been instituted in several ways, such as the form of a public nuisance low. This is when conditions cause discomfort, inconvenience, damage to property or injury from airlines fuels to cause air pollution. The governments have also intervened in the protection of the public to threaten the airlines' fuels emissions pollute air in the sky. As a result of much research, devices for pollution control have been developed, guidelines for air quality were established fuels tax increasing incentives were introduced to enforce ordinances for restricting the emission from airplanes' fuels. For example, governments can pass the clean air act, legislation to reduce air pollution in their countries. In conclusion, airlines can co-operate environmentally friendly management to prevent global warming, it is as a part of its corporate social responsibility and makes company wide efforts to do by saving energy and reducing aircraft fuel emissions. Hence, global airlines ought plan to achieve to reduce to consume excessive fuel emissions to reduce a narrowing of this gap between what consumers think and what they actually do concerned about the environment pollution was caused by airlines if which still wanted to make travelers who prefer to choose to go to travel by flying more than other water or ground transportation etc. methods.

How would a company , such as Easy Jet airline measure and monitor consumer's attitudes?

Easy Jet airline has created environment problems, e.g. harmful chemicals sift down from smoky trails of low-flying jets. The scream of Easy Jet airline engines is constantly heard by people who love near big city airports. It's aircrafts produce air pollution with consequent changes in climate.

It is a fact that many people prefer air travel rather than ground or water transportation, This has promoted a critical look at safety and quality control. Contributions to air pollution is a chief concern because of this revolutionary change in public transportation in the United States and around the world. The government must also establish standards for exhaust emissions. Thus, Easy Jet airline measure and monitor consumer's attitudes which needs to indicate to let them to believe that which suggests which airplane manufacturers are forced to develop low pollutant engines. Due to the problem of air pollution from its airplanes involve a complex set of interactions among technical, social and economic factors. Hence, it also needs to measure it's emission from Easy Jet aircrafts, particularly on landing and take offs, are a source of bitter complaints from nearby residents.

In a few airports visibility has been dangerously restricted by particulate emissions and photo chemical smog. Easy Jet airline also needed to have energy savings activities to its operations, ranging from procedural and flight plan improvement to reduce flight distance and attitude and weight management and it also needed to create energy through maintenance to achieve to continue to reduce co2 emissions by introducing high efficiency aircraft and through other measures to monitor consumers' attitudes . In line with its aim to be an environmentally friendly airline that harmonizes the needs of natural , humans and airline businesses. It aims to be respected by society , live up to its social responsibilities and make a contribution to society. Although emissions from aircraft are not included among greenhouse gas reduction targets, but it also needed to make systematic efforts to improve energy efficiency and reduce emissions by creating a road map to actively participate . Furthermore, Easy Jet airline also needed continually to pursue a management style that concerns nature, people and fellow corporations, even under the most severe conditions as a major practice toward implementing its environmental policy. Easy jet airline achieves environment goals to measure and monitor consumer's attitudes, such as minimizes energy and resource consumption and introduces up to date and fuel efficient fleet and engines and develops and apply energy efficient operation technique, it establish strict internal environmental standards to set internal standards that are stricter than general environment laws applied worldwide and minimize pollutants through systematic management and observance of standards. It systematically analyses the airlines' environmental impact and make the outcome to carry out reductions and evaluates the environmental impact of its aviation operations, maintenance and service and improves environmentally friendly processes and it continually improves environmental systems through feedback .

In conclusion, Easy Jet airline can increase the recycling of waste to reduce fuel consumption of resources and it can make systematic efforts to reduce emissions by creating a roadmap and actively participating in global warming by saving energy and reducing aircraft emissions through engine washing to aim to consume fuels efficiency and reduce emission to pollute air.

What might be the consequences for the marketing of a budget airline of Government policy measures which have the effect of doubling air fares in real terms?

If the country Government decided to raise higher flight fuel tax charge policy to budget airline. Due to the country Government hoped budget airline to reduce fuels consumption to provide to airplanes to use to reduce sky air pollution to cause global warning problem. In fact, budget airline needed to increase to use much fuels to provide to many flights to carry on passengers travel needs. Generally, budget airline would not like to choose to reduce to consume much fuels due to it's passenger numbers had been increasing. If budget airline decided to buy less fuels to reduce much fuels to consume for its flight needs. It would lose many passengers if it had not enough times of flights to provide airplanes to fly to different countries' airports to satisfy passengers' different flight route choices. However, the consequences for budget airline would also be passengers to choose to buy budget airline air tickets possibly if it decided to raise doubling air fares in real terms. Due to budget airline hoped to compensate its loss if it's country Government raised higher fuels tax to cause budget airline needed to pay high cost expenditure every year. Hence, budget airline needed to raise to spend two kinds of expenditure every year, such as purchasing more fuels expenditure and paying more fuels expenditure both. For long term, budget airline would choose to raise doubling or more air fairs in real terms in order to reduce to need to pay too much feel tax expenditure to compensate it's loss every year. In result, it's passengers would feel it's air tickets fares were not reasonable raised to compare it's other airline competitors, but it's flight services were not excellent to compare it's airline competitors specially. Hence, it's increasing air fares would cause many passengers to choose other airline competitors possibly.

Critically discuss how the marketing manager of a budget airline might respond.

Marketing manger might use cost benefit analysis to let budget airline to know how to invest in intangible asset, such as corporate social responsibility to give long term benefit to itself budget airline. I suggest this marketing manager needs to explain the reason why reducing fuel consumption is an investment in intangible asset to budget airline as below:

Airline transport has increasingly become a global technologically and dynamic growth industry. However, airline companies need to remain committed to satisfy the clients' growing demands in a sustainable manner when at the same time maintaining an optimal balance between economic progress, social development and environmental responsibility. The concept of corporate social responsibility is a challenge for who to face today's risky, competitive and complex airline business environment.

There has been a need for airlines in the airline industry to develop an environment agenda and take measures to minimize the ever increasing environmental impacts created by their activities. The forms of corporate social responsibility in the airline sector includes working in partnership with local communities, socially sensitive investment as well as involvement in activities for conservation of the environment. The fact, airlines are spewing 20% more co2 into the environment then previously estimated and there is a tendency for amount to increase to 1.5 billion tons a year by 2025 year. So, airline industry must need to innovative, environmentally responsible industry that drives economic and social progress. It has risks (social, environmental, operational, threat, strategic and financial risks) that they have to deal with marketing managers airlines, such as budget airline marketing manager is responsible for the optional decision making about corporate risks in its daily business. Adrian, (P. 2012) indicated that the marketing manager of budget airline needs to indicate the benefits can be categorized into three namely to let budget airline to feel as below:

(a) Regarding the economic view, budget airline is essential for facilitating world business and tourism, it needs to create jobs and enables the expansion of trade across the global by opening
up new market opportunities. It also attracts businesses to locations all over the world, hence satisfying the mobility requirement of a growing portion of the world's population. It also aids in the movement of products and services quickly over long distance facilities economies and social participation by remote communities.

(b) From the social perspective, budget airline forms an unique global transport network that links people in different countries safely and efficiently. Air transport is increasingly accessible to a large number of people who can now afford to travel by air for pleasure and its business purpose.

(c) Lastly, in terms of the environmental perspective, there is a need for budget airline to minimize or contain the impact in its environment through the continuous improvement of its

fuel consumption, noise reduction and the introduction of new technologies. Budget airline marketing manager can enquire this question to whose company, such as how budget airline can quantify the benefits derived from such investments to do with how to quantify the benefits, so budget airline can be compared to the cost of investments. Through budget airline has be different over the years to value many intangibles, such as corporate social responsibilities.

Budget airline marketing manager needs to make choices among several alternatives: it is important to adopt a tool that with allow choices to clearly weigh and distinguish between the options available. So, budget airline marketing manager needs to persuade whose company to believe to maximize the gain, which may be either economic or social and may be beneficial to an individual, a group or society at large, e.g. reducing fuel cost can maximize economic or social benefits for long term. The measurement of benefits from corporate social responsibility policy includes gains from additional income to an increased quality of life or a cleaner environment. On the other hand, the costs are made up of the opportunities forgone, internal and external costs and externalities. For instance, increasing the flying route for budget airline, the noise and air pollution are the externality when the secondary effect could be an increase in the cost operations. In this case, the pollution creates the new cost (

externality). The budge airline business cost is the increase in the cost of operating the additional route. The budget airline's fuel consumption causes air pollution will influence whose client stakeholders' powers of seeing and thinking, cultural setting, experience is from the past and motivation at the time of sensing to the airline image to be poor due to who will feel the budget airline is not a social responsible organization. It aims to earn profits from passengers, but it neglects to take care other stakeholders benefits due to its fuel consumption to pollute environment to cause global warming problem.

It seems that budget airline needs to considerate to use more fuel consumption to cause global warming problem more than doubling air fares in real terms if Government decided to raise more fuel tax charging to it to reduce its income.

I suggest marketing manager of a budget airline to reduce to use more fuels to pollute air, so budget airline does not decide to increase double air fairs charges to clients due to Government raises fuel taxation expenditure. Because it will cause clients to cancel its air tickets if who feel its air fairs are not reasonable to raise prices to compare other airline competitors. The marketing manager of a budget airline might respond to promote this navigation system to persuade budget airline does not choose to double air fares if Government raised fuel taxing charge. Innovation of flight operation on the optimum routes using (RNAV) Area navigation, as conventional airways and routes between airports were built by connecting ground navigation aids to the destination, the budget airline often became rather inefficient. On the other hand, RNAV can build routes connected any points with almost straight line by confirming aircraft position by means of global positioning system etc in addition to radio navigation destination of fuel consumption and CO2 emission through shortened flight time and distance. Other reducing fuel consumption include reduction of aircraft weight, use of new type point for aircraft painting to reduce emission of polluted to air . Hence, budget airline will spend less fuels to avoid to pay high fuels taxation expenditure to its Government and it does not need to charge double air fairs in real terms to cause many passengers who will choose to find other airlines to buy cheaper air tickets or who will cancel their budget airline air tickets due to who feel budget airline charges unreasonable air fairs. So, if budget airline did not achieve as above any methods to attempt to reduce fuel consumption, I believe that it will lose many passengers due to it decide to charge doubling air fares in real terms to compensate its fuel tax increasing expenditure .

What are the differences between multi level marketing and direct personal sale?

It seems that multi level marketing (MLM), netwrok marketing and direct sellers scheme marketing which are under the pyramid retail sales criterion. It means only third parties with no connection to the selling organizations are considered legitimate "ultimate users". Consequently, it deems the consumption of product by distributors (participants), "internal consumption" to be illegalitimate and simply a cover for fraud.

As multi level marketing or direct sellers from pyramid schemes both marketing which need individual participant or distributor who give money to buy their products to join to whose business to earn commissions. It seems the participant or distributor will be client role more than member or business partnership role. So, it seems MLM or direct sellers from pyramid schemes which main income sources are come from participants or distributors (internal clients). Rather, the key question is to determine whether the purchasers, whoever who may be actually resell or consume their products if the sales transactions are thus reveals to legitimate, as a matter of economic principle. They are also revealised to have increased social welfare. By accepting and adopting without further inquiry the "retail sales criterion", even though it is contrary to basic principles of economics and logic. Consequently, I shall indicate these above proposed test to distinguish legitimate from fraudulent enterprise of legitimacy to multi level marketing or pyramid schemes direct sellers both sale channels.

The reasons of legitimacy to multi level marketing or pyramid schemes direct sellers include which are inappropriately not just the consumer surplus flowing from, but also the profits that the parent firm earns from selling products to dustributors for their internal consumption. This error is caused by asserting that the resulting biased estimates of cash flow are sufficient to indicate that either a pyramid scheme (multi level or direct personal sale) is in progress. These both network sale channels discard all profits earned with internal consumption and because they assume, without the justificaton or validation, that all participants (distributors) in a direct selling enterprise act to as to maximize their cash income. What is the mean of relating high rate at which individuals are to direct selling is sufficient to be defrauded. It is alternative explanations for the rate at which individuals quit direct selling (the "quit rate"), and it provides no economic analysis or inquiry as to the quit rate those distributors might exhibit outside direct selling. It implies the quit rate of distributors in either direct selling or multi level (network) enterprise is pyramid scheme comparable to what one might observe in the counter-factual in which those individuals are employed as wage labour.

As the accounting theory view, pyramid multi level marketing fraud is considered of circumstances unrelated to pyramid fraud, such as calculations of distributors (participants) income whether a parent company's current cash outflows are fully funded by inflows. More direct personal sale or phyramid theme sale business calculations in this regard are biased toward finding fraud because which discard all profits earned with internal consumption and because which assume without theoretical justification or validation that all participants in a direct selling enterprise act as to maximize their cash income. Alternative explanation for the rate at which individuals quite direct selling the quit-rate and provides no economic analysis might exhibit outside direct selling. In fact, a high rate is sufficient to conclude that distributors (participants) were defrauded is apparent upon noting that there are also high quit-rates in other undeniably legitimate businesses. A direct selling (pyramid) of only a few distributors are able to build businesses that six and seven figure annual incomes is similiarly. Chief Executive officer and the distribution of salaries at many commercial entities exhibits a pyramidal form that logic would conclude that all corporations must be considered pyramid fraudsters in the labour market. Even of an economic analysis is well intentioned from direct personal sale market or pyramid enterprises in any countries. The politicies of different countries governments advocated and other misinterpretations, impose costs on consumers, producers and society at large. An objective appraisal of the costs and benefits with using test that are generated false positives represents the first step toward a meaning ful; analysis of the appropriate public policy.

This direct personal sale or pyramid direct sales scheme is concluded by providing an examination of the costs and benefits of regulation and increased enforcement. It seems direct personal sale market has no any legal doctrine support that only sales to third parties constitute legitimate business activity and application of logic and the misinterpretation and misapprehension of prior court rulings that have biased inquiries into the potential to generate false positives. So, some economists have failures of logic and economic that have characterized prior evaluations of public policy low and pyramid schemes or direct sale market.

Our goal is to providing some guiding principles to indicate economically sensible, how a true pyramid scheme or direct personal sale market can be identified and the costs and benefits of different approaches as to how fraud should be detected, with MLM and pyramid direct sale schemes. Otherwise, Multi level market, MLM compensates not only in the form of commissions on sales to distributors (participants), but it also compensate commissions on the sales of it's recurits. The fact, that the share prices of MLM enterprises that have one public have remained positive indicates that the market believes MLM enterprises have value and that this value will be sustained. In constrast, a direct personal sale market enterprise is unsustainable, e.g. a pyramid scheme that will collapse. Or always faces the threat of being shut down as a fraud by regulators, would not be able to sustain positive market value.

It is important to note that legitimate multi level network direct selling benefits not just the parent firm and distributors, but also businesses and society at large. A

MLM's products may require its salespeople to invest meaningful time and effort in educating the client as to the benefits of the product, resulting in a long sales cycle before sale is concluded. MLM provides the opportunity to every participant (distributor) to build to personal networks to introduce potential purchases to products. As a matter of economic principle of revealed preference or revealed profitability. Similarly, consumers who choose to purchase from legitimate MLM network direct sellers, they perceive more value in purchasing from a direct seller relative to other alternatives.

Many distributors join the MLM to purchase a preferred product at a lower price. Other distributors find MLM is a convenient way of support their income on their terms and according to their needs, for example by working why reasonally or part time. Another participants may find that participation in a entry point into a center or business opportunity to invest in their human capital and to acquire a network of business connections. Other participants may find that MLM (network selling) is the perfect match for their talents and skill sets. The goodwill to MLM is needed to concern. Consequently, consumer protection efforts have focused on identifying. Because, same MLM enterprises pretend to be legitimate direct sellers, such as fraudsters' debase the goodwill are trust that legitimate direct selling has established with consumers. Resultly, the direct personal sale enterprises pretend to do legitimate business activities to influence the unhealth or poor economic growth in societies. Otherwise, the Multi level market (MLM) or network market enterprises can do more legitimate business activities to influence the health or poor economic growth in societies.

However, muli level marketing , MLM is as a very popular

business model in the Western countries. It is a kind of the method of distribution of products. The method of building a sales network, it is one of the safest carries a very low risks ways of conducting business activity. The enter is to any markets, it is usually with market entry barriers and huge capital needs. Lack of expansion and lack of awareness of common practices. In the traditional business model, the risk of failure is very high. Also, unknown is the uncertain concerning the return on investments. However, despite high level of risk, this is the most popular business model.

So, multi level marketing is also called "network marketing". It is one of the fastest developing and still the least understand methods if introducing products to the market. It is mainly due to poor understanding of the system that multi level marketing is often regarded as network sales, pyramid sales or even pyramid schemes. It is marketing strategy and way of functioning of a company and its partners‘ independent distributors. Multi level marketing is a branch of direct sale. It involves offering products and services directly to clients on the basis of individual contacts, usually at direct's home, workplace or in other locations outside permanent retail sale branches. It is a form of sale outside, a traditional ship chain. It allows sellers to build personal structures of partners, who provide additional commissions from their sales. Every seller in multi level marketing has an opportunity to build own structure of salesman in which everyone is rewarded based on the marketing plan valid for each company. At the same time, achieving higher earnings, it is as a marketing strategy, way of functioning of a company and a system allowing to build individual network for independent distributors, classifying it has a branch of direct sales is a big mistake.

What is it's differences to pyramid scheme, MLM or network market and direct personal sale method? First, MLM is a retail sale, which is the most basic form of distribution carried out by means of a retail branch, e.g. grocery shop, chemist's shop department store, online auction site. Second, direct personal sale method is covering ususally the sale of insurance, kitchen wave houses etc. products. In this model of distribution commission from sold products goes only to the seller, who can't build network of his distributors. In order to sell products or services offered by a particular company, who has to be employed in the company as a sales representative. This means that who works for the owner of a company, the company's whose employer, thus the sales representative doesn't work for whose own benefit as in case of personal direct sale marketing. Third, direct personal sale marketing is transferring a product or service from the producer of service provider to the consumer. Otherwise, MLM, Multi level marketing is as a system of rewarding people who contribute to sale of products or provision of services. In the multi level marketing method people contributing to sale are those who recommend a purchase directly from a particular company. The employee whose is provided in course of making an order is rewarded for a recommendation resulting in actual sale, as the bonus system is usually multi level and allows generating passive income, income is not the direct effect of the work of recommending person. This works, this way is as every person has the opportunity to build individual consumer distribution structurer. In order words, multi level system rewards for directly recommended persons and recommended directly by direct ones. Fourth, MLM, it means mail order sale, this kind of distribution is characterized by lack of retail points in which products could be exchanged for money. The client makes an order directly in the company after learning about its offer on television, in telephone conversation or from a received catalogue. Finally, direct personal sale method is an illegal organization of sales, which is often mistaken for muti level marketing. One of the main reasons for an illegal organization is presented as a multi level system. The difference that makes pyramids illegal and multi level making legal is the inability to distribute a product or provide service. If there are no sales of a product, it is impossible to take about marketing companies by promising high sales convince participants to pay high one off about of money that allows then to participate in the programme which makes it impossible for participants to generate sales, as all payments go to the account of those organizing the business. Thus, direct personal sale is nothing like multi level marketing or network marketing . MLM, in which sale is always based on a product or service and the commission system rewards participants depending on the contribution, regardless of held position. So, MLM, it is a network created based on contacts and ties between people and the participation of all members of the network in this activity.

Can multi level lmarketing can assist organizational development ?

We can view multi level marketing from two perspectives, one of them is the point of view of concept, the producer or the company for which multi level marketing is one of possible ways of introducing a new product to the market bearing huge cost with promotion and without the need to transfer rights to a product to someone. The second perspective is the point of view of an independent distribution for whom multi level marketing is a model of business which doesn't require a concept or bearing the risk with investing capital, as in case of typical business activity or franchising, such an approach makes it possible to define MLM as method of distribution of products, in which costs associated with advertising and marketing are covered at the moment of actual sale. Sales are fueled by clients of the MLM company who use their contacts to recommend the purchase of particular products. The MLM company rewards the recommending person with a commission calculated based on the company's marketing plan for a recommendation ending with actual sale. Any marketing plan creates the possibility to generate unlimited revenues and at the same time eliminate risk with the necessity to invest substantial capital required to launch typical business activity.

How Multi level marketing can assist socio-economic development. For example, insurance business is a kind of MLM business, whether it can assist socio-economic development for long term. In insurance sector, insurance companies are looking for innovative methods to spread the message and maximum business in the short time. Many local MLM companies having quite large spread in the market with leading insurance brands to promote their insurance products along with their own products. Insurance sector makes available long time debt for the economic development of the country. At the same time, the MLM route provides employment opportunities and enhances their social status. The MLM members have opportunity to develop themselves personally. This multipe rise of MLM companies can be looked at as a social contribution and these insurance MLM companies or cooperatives are as a development oriented social movement. How insurance sector can assist the economic and social impact of MLM as a tool which can influence society through employment generation, mobilzing long term funds and improving quality of life of people. There has opportunity to attractive propective candidates to gain network marketing companies. Past studies indicated the fact that a 100 % annual turnover rate among sales personnel in certain network marketing company is not unusual. According to the Direct Selling Association in th United States, it indicated 70% of the revenue from the direct selling industry was generated by network marketing companies and most of this come from the better known companies, such as Amway, was multi level instead of single level compensation plans. Such as India, network marketing was in India during mid 90 year was followed by the establishment of the Indian arm of Amway corporation The total turnover of network marketing companies in India was estimated at $30,104 rising in 2005 year with an annual growth rate of 25%.

It seems Amway can assist USA Government to earn much taxation income and sale income to reduce USA unemployment rate. As, Amway exports to India market. Indian Direct Selling Association (IDSA) facilitates membership to build network marketing companies. So, India is a good network marketing for Amway MLM company. However, consumers often have negative perceptions of direct selling organizations and network marketing organization in particular. The aggressive selling techniques, exaggeration of facts in network marketing organization recruiting and pyramiding scams together toward a basis for this negative perception. Network marketing is a subset of direct selling and is also known as multi level marketing structure marketing or multi level direct selling. Network marketing can best be described as a direct selling channel that focuses heavily on its compensation plan because the distributors (members of the networks) may receive compensation in two fundamental ways. First, sales people (distributors) may earn compensation from their personal sales of products and services to the consumers (non-member of the network). Second, they may earn compensation from sales to purchase from those persons whom who have personally sponsored or recruited into the network (down lines), these down lines continue sponsoring or recruiting to the network sharing the benefits with their sponsors or recruiters (up lines). So, the aim of MLM network market which reward sales agents for buying products and selling products and finding other agents to buy and sell products. In common, the agents (distributors) or participants can earn marketings ranges from 20% to 50% of sales income. In addition, distributors can also receive a monthly commission for their personal volume which is the value of every product who personally buy or sell. Further, the distributors also receive a net commission on the sales of those who recruit into the networks. It seems that the sales developed network marketing are not developed from sales created by retailing, but also developed through recruiting or sponsoring independent distributors. Thus, as distributors continue to recruit or sponsor not distributors to expand whose network, the new distributors will contribute new sales to the network and gain commission in return. This hunge incentive makes the investment in insurance very attractive for a member. For example, coverage margin on first premium for insurance policies can earn the range of 30% to 40%. This given the leverage for structuring the insurance sale through MLM. MLM is a marketing function in which sales people are paid for their personal contribution as well as for the persons who recruit in to the function or process. Employees or sales people who are individual team to work from which who get a reward on the achievement sale force. So, who can sense much ideas to help marketing organizations to raise high demand when demand is too high and the current employees can't meet those are recruits come in the till the position. So, employees are encouraged to bring many employees to the organization.

MLM is also a very important function in providing jobs for the jobless. The recruitment process looks for young jobless people and earns them on income from which who can support themselves. It is happy feeling to know that you are working and at the same time providing opportunities for the loss fortunate to support them. You have chance to increase your paid if you introduce someone to work as participant or recruit or distributer role to any MLM market. It will reduce the numbers of unemployment of the insurance company in society. The idea presents people with great and better learning of the MLM strategy. When people are recruited in to the business, who are trained about its functions. This training acts as a good way of future advancements in the field. It also helps those individuals to use the knowledge to their advantage once who leave to job to enter marketing or sale career.

The job presents flexibility in hours work. Due people can work at any time who feel fits in them schedule. It can also train them to learn how to achieve whose sale target and attempt to do own business and no and captial spending. Is network marketing or multi level selling marketing as it is called all about getting rich quick with minimal effort?

Multi level marketing or network marketing means referring products or services directly to consumers within your network. It involves building a network. For each referral is made by the network. The preceding link or upline as those individuals are called in network marketing terms, gets a certain percentage of commission. MLM, network marketing doesn't need you to be a user of the product or service that you would eventally be referring within your network. Network marketing or MLM only need you put ability to put in lots of hard work. In fact, twice as much as in a regular job or business, willingness to learn new diversified skills, ability to discipline your ability to be as network with like minded people who can help you. So, MLM can help unemployment people to find either freelance or temporary or permanent kinds of position choices, such as sales person or distributor role in MLM company. So, network (MLM) marketing can offer various benefits to them like, lower initial costs of setting your business excellent training and product/service knowledge from industry experts, opportunity to earn additional residual income with a greater chance to move into a full time earned income model, flexibility to work at your own pace and time choice of retiring whenever you want.

Network market can be kind of multi level marketing. As network marketing is confronted with a number of issues that include the continuous erosion of campaign effectiveness, the fragmentation of traditional markets, the disappearance of the vendors' information advantage and significant changes in the distribution channel. Based on established building blocks of marketing and social network theory, a conceptual framework called network theory to integrate the two fields in a systematic way.

The networked marketing framework provides a structure

for identifying the customer social network's impact on the marketing effectiveness in the different customer lifecycle phases and suggests the use of certain tools to acqire knowledge about the nature and the functional details of the social influence. However, the network marketing framework was tested in a setting on an international sample of a large company's customer database. How customer social network activity with an impact on marketing is the most intense in the purchase phase and the least. Hence, in the awareness phase, as well as the fact, that product and communication are the mix areas most impacted by social networks. For example, health care is an individual necessity and kind of national luxury product of a kind of multi level decision models. Due to health care is neither a necessity or a luxury, it is both since the income elasticity varies with the level of analysis. With insurance, individual income elasticities are typically near zero, when national health expenditure elasticities and commonly greater. It is to expected that measured income elasticities will differ for an individual, a risk-pooling group, or a national health system, just as price elasticities for individual, firm and market demand normally differ from each other. In past, some economists indicate income elasticity of individual, health expenditures under insurance (usually 60% to 95% of total spending) is typically near zero or negative, when the elasticity of national health expenditures with respect to national income is typically greater than 1.0. So, it seems individual income level and health factor has close relationship to decide to buy any health insurance policies.

Whether how multi level decision model quickly resolves to make evident the role of social and private insurance in linking micro and macro analysis in health economics.

Within an insurance group, the bulk of the health resources will be allocated to those individuals who are ill and to get benefits from medical care. Individual budget constraints and ability to play concerns are pooled insurance financing. The contrast between the behaviour of the average individual, and the behaviour of the group to buy medical health insurance mean is well illustrated by insurance. However, medical health insurance pools are not only likely to display separation between group and individual behaviour, who are designed to bring about such a separation. The purpose of medical health insurance is to remove the individual budget constraint, and to reduce or eliminate the influence of cost of care on patient's and physician's decisions of how much care to use. If persons are fully insured, correlations with measures of individual income provide no information about income effects per each, e.g. the effect of monetary budget constraints, but instead reflect the influence of other unmeasured variables, cost of time, family resources, education, preferences etc. that are correlated with an individual's income. Hence, it seems that multi level model of determinants of pyramid or network sale method is suitable to sell in health insurance market. In any country's health insurance market, it will have two kind groups of people who will feel who have need to buy health medical insurance product. One group is without purchase any health medical insurance product , and another group owns health medical insurance product . At the macro level, income effects are still strong to influence anyone to decide to buy health medical insurance product, but variation factor due to differences in health status can also influence anyone to decide to buy health medical insurance product . With the country's people who feel need of health medical product, the pooling of funds will remove the insurance market income constraints and tends to strengthen the correlation of individual health status with expenditures. However, individual income effects still dominate the insurance market in the health medical insurance any country. So, it seems that health medical product insurance will have large share to lead to any country's insurance product income among of the travel insurance, accident insurance, life insurance, car insurance, employee welfare insurance etc. different kinds of insurance products market in any country. So, mulit level marketing shall be suitable to enter insurance product sale market.

Direct sale represents a modern product distribution system directly to consumer. Generally, directly to their homes, to their workplace or other places, besides retail shops. Ths best known type of direct sale, the network marketing or multi level marketing implies the existence of a network of distributors which earn income from selling on commission, to which who add the trade marketing. So, insurance, travel agent, share broker, property agent etc. these occupations which can belong to multi level or network marketing.

Following, I shall discuss the another kind of multi level marketing, e.g. franchise business. Franchise means the field of activity in which it was used. It is a license allowing the designee to sell and market a company's products or services in a particular place, using the name or the trade mark of the company, e.g. Mc Donald fast food restaurant. It allows whom to do business for the franchise owner, but not through the franchise owner. From the marketing point of view, franchise represents a distribution system based on the partnership between two parties which are legally independent. Between the franchisor (the proprietary owner, the owner of the trade mark of products and services) and the franchisee. However, developing a franchise using a well known trade mark, so it is a more complex distribution system in multi level marketing view point. Also, franchise business can be sold from internet sale channel in the multi level marketing technological view point.

FIVE

How Time Influences Consumer Behavior

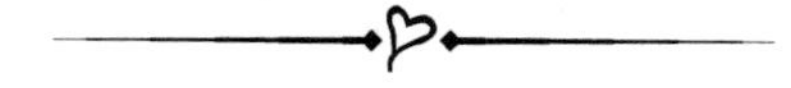

Can time pressure influence influence consumer behavior ?

How and why time pressure can influence consumer behavior? To research time how influences consumer behavior, it has different theory to explain why and how the consumer is influenced to make the choice by different factors. For example, utility theory,it explains that consumers make choices based on the expected outcomes of their decisions. They are viewed as rational decision makers and they only consider self interest.

Utility theory views consumer is as a " rational economic man". However, the factors influence consumer behaviors may include these activities, such as need recognition, information search, evaluation of alternatives, the building of purchase intention , the act of purchasing choice, consumption and finally disposal. Hence, it seems that all the consumer's activities in whose purchase processes. They will influence their choice. For example, when the property purchase consumer , he plans to research different kinds of properties information concern price, location, housing areas, room numbers, building facilities and environment facilities. He will find some sample target properties information to make comparison in order to decide to buy which of property is the most suitable to satisfy his living need.

However, it is not only one activity for the property purchase buyer in his decision making process. It also include evaluation of alternatives activitiy when he ensures the accurate property information number in order to evaluate whether which one of all these property choices is the most suitable one. Hence, it explains that property information research and evaluation of alternatives both activities are needed to spend much time for this property buyer. If he does not plan to find one property to live in short time, it is possible that he can spedn one month, even more than one month or more than three months time to do the only property information gathering activity.

Hence, it seems that time factor is not the main factor to influence the property buyer to do property purchase decision immediately. Otherwise, if the property buyer plans to find one new property to live within one month. Then, time factor is possible one important factor to influence this property purchase chocie decision. For example, if he felt that he needs more time to spend to gather information concerns the large house area size and the properties have more than three bathrooms and/or bedrooms properties information. Then, he will be possible not to find any this kinds of all property information. So, it means that all these properties won't be his choice. It is because long time property information gathering activity factor influnce.

I assume that the property buyer is a economic man and he does not spend much time to do the property information gathering activity. So, this kind of property needs him to spend long time to gather properties inforation in order to make this kind of properties comparison. Moreover, because he expects to live one new property within one month. So, he only chooses the properties, they have less than three bedrooms and/or bathrooms to gather sample properties information in order to make property purchase decision within one month. Hence, the time variable factor can only influence the property purchaser when he/she needs to make decision to buy one new property to live in the short time. If some kinds of properties choices number has a lot and the property buyer feels to let that he/she must need to spend long time to find the suitable properties number to make evaluation alternatives comparison behavior.

Then, the time variable limiting pressure factor will be possible the main factor to influence the property buyer's choice in order to make the most suitable kind of property purchase decision. Hence, it is one case example of how time limiting pressure factor can influence consumer purchase choice decision, such as property purchases market case. The reason explains why the property buyer needs to spend time to do property information gathering.

I assume that general property buyer behave rationally in the economic sense. They won't only believe property agent individual property photos advertisement , it concerns where the property location is and facility etc. information on property photos in order to evaluate whether the property price is reasonable to pay. Generally, property buyers need to attempt to gather property information and visit the different actual property locations to make choice. So, general property consumers would have to be aware of all the available different kinds of properties consumptin options from themselves properties information gathering and the properties agents' verbal properties introduction both be capable of correctly rating each property alternative and the available to select the optimum course of the final property purchase action.

Hence, in the property purchase and sold market, limiting time pressure factor will be important influential factor to decide whether the kinds of properties will be option to some property buyers when they feel need to find one suitable property to buy in short time. Otherwise, in some food consumption market , time limiting pressure factor will not be the main factor to influence consumer option. Such utility theory indicates consumers are as one rational economic man, whom do not expect to spend much time to do any options evaluation decision making.

However, in coffee market, buying a coffee comes almost automatically and does not need much information search. Hence, time limiting pressure factor won't one main factor to influence coff consumer to choose to buy the kind of coffee to drink. However, there are other factors to influence coffee consumers' kind of coffee drinking option from cultural, social, personal or psychological factors. So, coffee taste producer can follow these factors to estimate how coffee consumers might behave in the future when making any kinds of coffee making purchasing decisions.

Firstly, social factor can affect coff consumer behavior significantly. Every coffee consumer has someone around influencing his/her coffee buying decisions. The important social factors include reference groups, family, role and status , e.g. when the coffe buyer has high income job and his friends have good educational level and high income. Then, he will compare his reference group, such as his friends' coffee buying behavior choosing which kinds of coffee taste to drink in habits or lifestyles. If he chooses the kind of coffee taste to drink, its price is cheaper to compare his friends' drinking coffee tastes. Then, he may be influenced to follow his friends to drink the same kinds of coffee taste in order to keep their same social status and role between him and his friends.

Secondly, the coffee consumers will be influenced how to choose which kinds tastes of coffee to drink by personal factors, such as his age, life cycle state, occupation, economic situation , lifestyle and personality and self-concept. Age related factors are such as taste in food, e.g. the kinds of coffee taste. Although, coffee price is cheap, but if the coffee consumer's income is more and he/she can often spend to buy different kinds of taste coffees to drink. Then, his/her income level will have much purchasing power to influence his/her purchasing behavior. Hence the coffee consumer's frequency of consumption of different kinds of coffee taste drinking choice behavior will represent whether his/her income level is high or low in possible. For example, the consumer needs to go to automatic coffee shop to buy at least three cups or more different kinds of high class good taste coffee brands to drink per week. Although, these high class coffee brands' prices are higher than the low class of coffee brands. But the coffee consumer still only buys any one of these kinds of high class brands' coffee taste to drink. Hence, it seems that this coffee consumers ought have high income to let hims to buy at least three cups of high class brand of coffee taste to drink from automativ coffee ship per week.

So, income factor can influence the coffee consumer to choose either coffer purchase from supermarket or coffee drinking at automatic coffee shop. If the coffee consumer only chooses to buy coffee from supermarket, due to the bottles of different kinds of brand coffee can provide more different tastes of coffees choices from shelves to let him to buy to drink at home. So, it seems that the coffee consumer's income level is low in general. Otherwise, if the coffee consumer only chooses to go to automtic coffee shop to buy the high class brands of coffee tastes to drink at least thre times or more per week. It may mean that the coffee consumer has high income level to support him/her to often go to automatic coffee shop to buy different kinds of high class coffee tastes to drink frequently every week. Som high or low income level factor can influence every coffee consumer individual drinking coffee behavioral options.

Moreover, when the coffee consumer is younger coffee consumer will be possible to buy much coffee to drink. Because younger age people can accept to drink coffee habitually more than older age people. Also, it is possible that younger peopler feel often drinking coffee behavior will help them to bring more health feeling and /or raising nervous to learn , due to they need often to go to schools to study. Otherwise, older age people feel often drinking coffee behaviors won't help them to bring more health and they do not need to raise nervous to learn.

Finally, even, cultural difference factor will influence coffee consumers number fo any countries. For example, western countries'people like to drink any kinds of coffee tastes traditionally. Asia countries' people like to drink any different kinds of teas tastes traditionally. So, different kinds of teas tastes will be asia people's traditional drinking substitute to replace different kinds of coffee tastes more easily. Hence, culture difference will be one factor to influence asia coffee buyers number. So, it seems that time limiting pressure factor won't influence coffee consumers' coffee taste choices to different kinds of high class or low class brands, visiting coff shops or visiting supermarkets choices, frequent or not frequent coffee drinking behaviors.

How can sellers persuade consumers to choose to buy their products or consume their services in time pressure environment easily?

It is a valuble research topic to concern how to know how consumer individual decision making to spend his/her available resources (time, money and efforts, or consumption relatd aspects) as well as how any why he/ she chooses the preference brand to buy its any kind of products or consume its services, when he/she chooses to buy the brand of products or consume its services? Hence, marketers need to obtain an indepth knowledge of consumer buying behavior.

In any buying process, time factor will have about 10 % to 40 % to influence consumer decision. When the consumer feels hurry to consume, e.g. planning to go to travel, when he/she needs to choose to buy which airline's air ticket and what day and time is the right air ticket prebooking purchase decision right time choice; or enrolling which school to be choosed course to study decison, e.g. how long time is needed to be choose which school is the most suitable to provide the most suitable courses studying choce change; purchase warm clothes to wear in winter, when is the suitable time to choose to buy the cheaper warm clothers to prepare to wear in winter, e.g. Jan to Mar.,

April to June, July to Aug. month; when is the most suitable time to buy another new house to live, when the property consumer(buyer) has lived present house for long time, e.g. three years or more. All of these issues will include time factor to influence the consumer feels when he/she ought choose to buy the kind of product or consume the kind of service. However, the other factors will also include to influence his/her decision, e.g. family, friend relationship factor, advertising factor, social status factor, cultural difference factor, personal psychological need level or satisfactory level factor, young or old age factor, income level factor, economic environment factor, material enjoyable need factor etc. factors.

However, time pressure factor will be the consumer individual intrinsic (internal) psychological feeling factor, and it is the consumer individual intrinsic feeling to judge whether when he/she ought spend some money to buy the kind ofcnew product or the kind of consume service (what time is the most reasonable or the most suitable time) to make purchase choice decision. However, when the consumer feels hurry to make purchase decision. So, he/ she will not hope to spend more time to gather more information to compare and evaluate which one is the right brand of product tochoose to buy or the right service to consume among different brands of products or services. Otherwise, if the consumer has more time or he/she can make the decision to buy any brand of product. Then, he/ she ought spend more time to gather more information to compare and evaluate which one is the most suitable product choice to buy or which one is the right service choice to consume. So, time pressure factor will have some influence to any consumers to make decision about what time is the suitable time to buy the kind of product or consume the service. For example, heater product is usually when winter weather time, the heater products need number ought increase in winter weather time or season. But, it is possible that the heater products need number won't increase in winter season / weather possible, when one country , there are many householders or families , they have one heater number at least at home. Then, it is possible that these householders or families won't have consumption desires to buy one more heater product to use in winter at home, because they have had one heater to use at home in winter. So , when the country has have many customers number, they are using the kind of heater products at homes. Most people own at least one heater number factor will have possible to influence enough time available to cause they do not feel hurry to buy any heaters to use at homes, so, their do not feel time pressure to buy any heaters in short time. Because they do not plan to buy the kind of product to use at home in short time when they have one heater product at least to use at homes in present. Hence, it brings this question: How to attract or persuade the customers, they are using the kind of product to let they feel time pressure to make decision to buy another new or same brand of product to replace to use? The product's better quality , long durable time useful, brand loyalty and past good purchase experience factors will influence him/her to feel time pressure to need to buy another new product in short time. So,when the consumer feel time pressure to make decision to purchase, he/she will choose when is the most right time to gather information, search, select, use and dispose of another new product to replace the old product in the short time.

Hence, the brand of product needs have good product motives, may be raised to the consumer's impluse, desires, considerations which make the buyer purchase the brand's new product to replace the present using product in order to achieve whose satisfactory needs to emotional product motives and rational product motives both. Moreover, persuading or encouraging the consumer feels he/she has real need to buy the kind of new product or replace the present old product (s), the brand of product marketer needs let the consumer feels these any one of nature of motive to raise his/her purchase decision desire in time pressure environment. The natures of motive may include: When the consumer feels desire for saving money, he/she will choose to buy it when the brand of product falls down, when he/she feels fear to be sickness, retirement, he/she will choose to buy insurance policy, when he/she feels pride, or high social status knowledgement, he/she will buy premium product , e.g. gold, expensive watch, car , when he/she feels fashion need, he/she will move house to live from rural to urban, or rural people imitate urban to learn to do their fashion living behavior, when he/she feels possession need, he/she will feel need to buy antiques for its future unique worth satisfactory feeling in possible, when he/she feels health need, he/she will choose to buy health foods, join memebership in health clubs, when he/she needs to enjoy comfortable feeling, he/she will feel need to buy micro-oven, washing machine to use at home, when he/she feels love and affection need, he/she will buy gift items to give to whose friends or families for presents in their birthday or lover day etc. special days to let they to feel happy. So, when the marketer can touch the consumer individual different nature of motives to satisfy his/her personal purchase feeling need and it can know how to influence them to feel that they have these any one of purchase motive needs in short time. Then, they will be persuaded to raise time pressure to make purchase decison to buy any kind of products in short time.

However, instead of attractive good product quality method can attempt consumers to make time pressure consumption behavior. The another method is brand loyalty building method, which can be attempted to encourage or persuade consumers to feel consumption desire need to make decision to buy the brand of any products in time pressure consumption environment. For example, when the consumers feel the brand is loyalty and it can build good image to his/her feeling , and this time pressure factor can inlfuence this brand of any products which has high discount price to attract the consumer individual attention , e.g. familiar brand high class cars, the good confident house agent's high class houses, and the expensive and infrequently buying items, come under this category. When their prices are fallen down to sell cheaper , e.g. twenty per cent discount or more than twenty percent discount sale price than the other similar competitive brands' any products' normal prices. Then, it is possible to let these expensive items' consumers have high involvement and high feeling need in time pressure consumption environment. Because they assume that this discount sale price will be short time sale price, e.g. after three months or next month etc. short time discount sale price in short time period. Then, these expensive items' prices will be raised to the normal sale price, even higher price. so, they have time pressure feeling to feel that it is right time to make consumption decision in order to avoid to lose these low price purchase benefit in this unpredictive cheap discount price purchase items. so, if the expensive item marketer can build long time good brand loyalty relationship to consumers. Then, it will have much influential effort to persuade consumers feel consumption desires need by its any extensive items in the unpredictive short term discount period, due to they do not want to loss this large discount purchase price chance. So, short time discounted sale price, it is another method to persuade consumers to choose to buy the brand's any products in short time pressure consumption environment.

The another persuading time pressure consumption method is that it can let consumers to think more habitual buying the kind of products. products like stationery, groceries, food etc. fall under this category. For example, when the consumer fees the brand of any products ,he/she has habitual purchase experience, of he/she feels that the brand's any products won't sell in market temporary, even he/she can not buy it to use again. Then, it is possible to infuence him/her to feel immediate purchase need to buy a lot of product or food number to keep to use or eat later in the time pressure environment, e.g. the food consumer buys the brand of any breads to eat in supermarkets habitually, but in this moth, he/she watchs TV advertisement to be acknowledge this brand of any breads won't be bought from any supermarkets as soon as possible. Hence, it is possible to influence him/her to plan to make choice to buy a lot of number of this brand of any breads in order to keep the enough of this brand of breads number to eat later. So, this brand of any breads sale loss in supermarkets that will cause the habitual food consumers of this brand of breads, whom make consumption choice to buy a lot number of this brands any breads in short time suddenly. Because they are eating this brand of any kinds of breads habitually. They feel much eating need to lot number of this brand of any breads in short period, because it can satisfy their habitual taste needs of this brand's any kinds of breads. So, brand loyalty and habitual consumption to the kind of product or food , ehich will result simply from the habit and it can influence the consumers feel consumption need to buy the brand's any kinds of products or foods when they feel that they may not buy it again or they can not earn discount advantage after the short time. So, any one of these sale strategies will have possible to raise the consumer individual consumption desire to the brand of products in the short time pressure consumption environment. Also it needs to spend much time to gather information in order to make purchase decision, because the brand had built confidence to consumers when they feel this brand's any products or foods are better to compare the similar brands' any products or foods habitually. So, time pressure consumption environment will persuade them to feel consumption desire to buy this brand's any products or foods in short time. When, they fer that they can not buy any more for this brand's any kinds of products or foods or discounting price in this final short purchase time.

In conclusion, these factors can influence consumer behaviors to be changed to feel time pressure need to do purchase decision making behavior from encough time gathering information available feeling behavior. They have these same views, e.g. habits and routines are very influential, particularly for behaviors repeated daily in a semi-automatic fashion. The consumer's past purchas experience to the brand's products, positive or negative emotion to the brand's products, and the brand's familization, recognition are strong influence , the information available , it is the consumer's mind and the relative important information given to let the consumer knows form different advertisement medias matters for decision making, greating between pieces of information and can be influenced by personal psychological timing limited pressure, the consumer's comparison to differences in price or other characteristics, many pursue value (or in bargain), and compare to alternatives or past knowledge, consumer personal greater value on the immediate future and heavily disocunt future costs or savings to the brand of product, feeling simple and easy decision making process to the product , it can lead the consumer to avoid to spend long time to make purchasing decision and the consumer will easy to choose to buy the product when he/she feels have a loss value if he/she does not decide to buy the product in the short time. SO, it seems that when the marketer can motivate the consumer's consumption desire to feel saving money, promote health, avoid waste time and less nervous workload to gather information for comparison and evaluation alternatives aim. It is seen favorably by the consumer personal time pressure purchase decision making and sense of justice influence factors.

However, sociologists have categorised the motives for consumption behaviors in the short time by the fundamental consumption decision making needs or wants which they satisfy, e.g. having a clear understanding what benefits, characteristics, economic value to the brand's any products , feeling consumption decision making process is a leisure activity. These drivers for consumption behaviorw will either bring positive or negative to influence the consumer personal emotion, either owning enough time available or time pressure environmental impacts can be seen to influence whether the consumer feels he/she needs how long time to be spent to make comparison and evaluate alternatives in order to make final purchase choice in whom decision making process. Hence, the consumer himself/herself time pressure consumption decision making feeling, it can bring positive purchase choice influence,when the marketer can build brand loyalty to let many consumers to feel in the market. Otherwise, if the marketer can not build brand loyalty to let many consumers to feel, but consumers feel time pressure to compare and evaluate its any products to other similar brands of products in the competitive market. Then, its products may be not the preference choices the many customers among the different brands of products choices. So, building long time brand loyalty relationship to satisfy consumers' needs, it will bring positive preference purchase choice to raise the sale effort to the brand of any products when consumers need to make purchase choice in time pressure consumption environment, e.g. seasonal discount sale period, products or foods shortage supply period, without any forever sale possibility in market. Hence , it seems that brand loyalty building factor will influence any brands of products /foods /service sale or provison number to be raised or reduced in possible. Also, it can explain why and how it has close cause and effect relationship between time pressure consumption environment and the brand loyalty building to the brand of products/foods/services to any marketers nowadays.

Can customer purchase experience influence business success?

In general, we argue that the ability to achieve business success by focusing on the physical aspects of the product, e.g. quality, price or the delivery. We are less considering the feeling aspects of our customer purchase experience. Many businessmen do not understand salespeoples' sale behavior can influence any customer how to feel the brand's products image. Why can influence customer experience bring any business success. Generally, in consumption market, customers have similar products, similr salespeople, similar technology and similar pricing to choose to buy any kinds of products. Hence, how to influence customer experience, will let the customer feels good or bad image to the company as well as repeating purchase choice to the company's products again.

Customer expertise means the customer emotion whether he feels good or bad to the brand's product quality, reliability, pricing. It is not just about the company's salespeople services, it is about sales, marketing, web site design, systems, processes and overall staffs performances. Customer experience is differentiating solely on the traditional psysical elements, such as price, delivery, and lead times is no longer a business strategy. The customer experience is that differentiation. What is the best customer experience, e.g. in a shop, on a vacation, at a restaurant, on a flight? Any of these different consumption environment, which will influence any customer feels different consumption experience. However bad customer experiences are easy to produce.

A great customer experience can excit good customers' emotion. There are two elements to a consumer experience: The physical and the emotion. We are all human beings : Emotions are constant. They are there all the time. I believe that emotion side of the customer experience is the essence of first direct to compare the price of a product, its quality, the lead times for delivery. For a customer to put eh phone down, or click off the internet and not only know that something has been sorted, but feel good about it. These environment factors can influence the customer's purchase emotion will have long or short time of good or bad feeling to the product, e.g. within a week or two, the food is consumed and that experience has gone. For a car company, the consumer is living with his brand for up to three or four years following the day he bought the car. So, long or short customer emotion time, it depends on whether the product can be used how long. For restaurant example, when the restaurant's competitors can raise similar taste of foods, similar price, similar restaurant environment, e.g. size, location, design.

The competitive factor will be emotion factor, how to let its food customers feel satisfactory and comfortable and kindly waitors' serving feeling in order to bring short time good (positive) or bad (negative) emotion feeling after every had eatten all foods and prepare to pay money, till to leave the restaurant's whole eatting consumption time. So, it seems that emotion factor can influence whether food customers will repeat choose the restaurant to eat again. If the restaurant can let many customers to build short time good emotion feeling when they choose this restaurant won't loss many old food customers easily. Even they willl help it to persuade their friends to choose this restaurant to eat. Hence, customer serving experience will be one important factor to influence this restaurant's success, when it has many similar food taste, similar price, similar restaurant environment design and locations' competitors existence.

For product sale industry example, in general, manufacturers will focus on physical experience, e.g. price, availability, accessibility, efficiency , ease of use, range and delivery. They feel emotion experience is not important. For this suitation example, when one client had bought one computer from the computer shop. He brings it to home to use. Suddenly, we feel that this computer has some engineering functions, he does not know how to use, but he had left this computer ship to enquire its salespeople. If this shop company has one enquiry department, its staffs can answer any technical issues concern how to use this company's any function, due to any buyers can phone telephone hotline and it takes time to establish a call centre operation to let them to enquire , any computer function technical problem in order to any computer function technical problem in order to ensure their any problems correctly. Then they will have more food emotion, due to this company shop can improve its customer satisfaction for any technical problems in order to get solutions immediately from its call centre computer technician assistance service. Hence, this computer shop's sale after service will be one important factor to bring good customer purchase experience.

In general, the physical customer experience for either service provision or purchase business stages will follow as below:

Step one: The customer expectation to the product or service is setted by advertising, brand image, personal relation, word of mouth.

Step two: The consumer will make pre-purchase interacton, either quotes or information gathering.

Step three: When the consumer has choose to buy which brand of product or consume whom service provider, he will make purcahse interaction, ordering, activities and final purchase implementation.

Step four: After the consumer pays money to buy the product or consume the service, he will make evaluation, to using and consuming the product/service, it is post purchase interaction.

Step five: Post-experience review, it is intuitive review, customer experience and revise experience and expectation. It is the most important factor to influence the customer's emotion whether his feeling is good or bad after he used the product or consume the service. It is one most important customer experience final stage. Because this stage will influence whether the customer will choose to repeat to buy the shop's products to use again or consume the shop's service again.

During this restaurant's final customer experience stages, its physical and emotion both expectations will influence whether you , such as this restaurant food cusomer will be influenced to choose to eat its food again in the short time by your good emotion influence. I shall indicate this situations: In you order your food stage, the restaurant can provide the choise is adequate physical expectation and the server engages you in a discussion and is excited by the meal choice to your emotion expectation. In you need wait for your food to arrival stage, it can provide approprite length of the phsical expectation and it's sufficient time not to feel rushed in your emotion expectation. In your food arrival stage, you feel that it is the food you ordered and it looks appetising physical expectation and the server is smiling in your emotion expectations. In your eating food stage, you feel it is the correct temperature physical expectation and the sensations are pleasant in your emotional expectation. In your asking for your bill stage, you feel this is not as important as serving other customers physical expectation and the server smiles and hurries to get the bill emotional expectation. In your bill arrival stage, it takes an appropriate amount of time to time physical expectation and you expect it to be value foe money emotion expectation. In your leaving the restaurant stage, it provides you are thanked for coming physical expectation and you can also feel that you have a warm feeling they linked you being there emotion expectation. Finally, in your walking back to your can final stage, you feel that it doesn't cause you feel inconvenience or needing to pay extra car park fee, due to your choice to eating this restaurant's good, when you feel car park is still well to your physical expectation and you feel safe in your emotion expectation. So, all of your food consumption in this restaurant's all stages can build good physical and emotional expectatons to satisfy your great customer experiences, during your short time eating process in this restaurant. Hence, this restaurant will let you feel good emotion, due to your hope can be met and exceed you positive expectations from this restaurant's service, exceed its negative service expectations and it can identify opportunities to exceed your mininal level physical expectations and emotion expectations to this restaurant.

On conclusion, nowadays customer experience factor will be more important to compare other factors to influence any businesses success. Due to customer individual good or bad emotion will be influenced by his/her post-purchase experience influence. Businessmen can not neglect how to satisfy their customers' past- good purchase experience feeling and building good emotion. It will be one important successful factor to compare other physical factors.

May time dominate consumption final purchase decision making ?

Whether can time limited pressure dominate consumer individual to make more rational purchase decision? Can the consumer make more rational decision , when he/she has enough time to make final purchase decision? I shall explain why and how the consumer can make more rational decision when he/she has enough time as well as

I shall explain that without time pressure environment. It may dominate consumers to make more rational or more accurate decision making.

I assume that it is the final time limited pressure day to nee the consumer to spend more nervous do time final purchase decision among the different kinds of similar products choices, e.g. air conditions . If the consumer decides that the day is the final purchase decisin to choose to buy one air conditin among these different brands of similar air conditions in the super store. So, if on the that day, he/she can not make any final decisin to choose which brand of air condition to buy on that final consumption day in the super store when the super store visitor sees the final air condition consumption day advertisement in this year in this super store . Then, he/she won't buy any air condition again if he/she can not buy on that day in this super store.

The another time dominates immediate purchase behavior is that I assume that one common air condition can not be bought in short time later if all air condition consumers can not make decision to buy any air condition in this super store. So, his/her personal time limited pressure can dominate whose final or condition purchase decision in this super store on that day. If the store has many different brands of air conditions to lead him/her to spend long time to compare which is th best worth to buy in this super store. Then, it will let him/her to feel difficult to make the air condition final purchase decision in the store on that day. Otherwise, if the super store has less different brands of air conditions to need him/her to spend less time to compare which is the best worth to buy in the store. Then, he/she may make the final air conditin purchase decision making more easily on that day.

So, the final air condition purchase day of the super store, the super store's air condition final day's time can dominate the air condition buyer to make air condition purchase decision immediately. Due to he/she feels that all of these day brands air conditions can not bought from this super store after that day. So, he/she needs to make the air condition purchase decision making in this super store on that final air condition purchase day in this year. Because it is the final air condition purchase day in this super store of all sir conditions products. If he/she can not make the choice to buy any one brand of air condition in this store. Then, it is possible that he/she will lose this store's final cheap price air condition purchase benefits. However, if this super store has too many brands of air conditions need him/her to choose. It will cause him/her to spend more time to choose. Consequently, it will cause he/she feels difficult to compare which brand of air condition is the best and he / she does not choose to buy any one in this super store.

Hence, this super store ought have less number different brands of air conditions to let every air condition consumer to choose in order to let they can make final air condition purcahse decision on this air condition cheap price purchase final day. So, less different number brands of air conditions will dominate the consumers to spend less time to make purchase decision immediately and easily on that final sale day in this super store. Hence, it seems that the super store's final air conditions sold day time will dominate many air condition visitors to make purchase decision when they visit this super store in summer season on that day in this super store. Because all this super store's air condition consumers do not expect that they can not buy the best quality of air conditin in this super store final sold day , due to air condition stocks number shorten challenge is not supplied enough on that final cheap purchase day in this super store. Consequently, that time pressure will increase to influence them to make the final air condition purchase decision in the final sold day‘ s short time, before this super store closing time on that day. Their time pressure feeling comes from the super store 's air condition number shortage supply in possibility. It will dominate them to make the final air condition purchase decision in this super store in short time.

The anothe time dominates immediate purchase behavior case is that I assume that one common picture painter(actor), he finds one architect to help him to build one house. The architect only needs to folloe his house picture to build one house. The common picture painter tells him that he will give him building expenditure and building profit after he helps him to build the house profit after he helps him to build the house successfully. After six months, the architect made one decision, he did not demand the famous picture painter paid him for the building service fee. But, he needed him give the house picture to him to replace the building service fee. Because the picture painter feels that he didn't need to pay the building service fee to him to buy the architect's building service in these six months building time. Hence, he accepted his offer to give his common house picture to the architect for his reward.

I assume that this six months time dominate the architect to make the final building service fee decision either acceptance the common picture painter customer's building service fee or acceptance his common house picture replaces the building service fee. However, the architect believes that this common house picture can have higher selling price to compare his building service fee income. Consequently, I assume that his evaluation is right, this house picture selling price is more than three times to compare his past six months's building service income. So, it proved that his choice is right, because he could earn more than three times of his building service income after he decided to accept the common picture painter's this house picture to attempt to sell it in the picture auction market. It seems that this six months long house building time can dominate these both buyer and seller's purchase and selling behaviors, such as this picture painter and this architect. When the architect has this six months enough time to let the picture painter to change his building service offer decision from building service fee payment to his common house picture offer exchange. This architect can achieve his intention to let him to accept his free house picture sold product exchange offer more easily. Otherwise, if the architect can not need six months to build this house, he only needs three months or less time to build this house, then it is possible that the picture painter won't accept his this house picture offer to replace his building service fee easily. If he considers that whether his this house picture's selling price has possible to sell higher price to compare this building service fee for this house picture. He will choose to sell this house picture himself. Hence, due to the picture painter can not sell this house picture in this past six months. So, in this six months period, the house painter can not sell this house picture in picture auction market. This six months period can dominate his low market worth selling feeling to this house picture as well as it can influence him to make this house picture exchange decision to replace his house service fee.

The picture painter will ask himself, ought the house picture painter need to wait how long time to sell this picture in auction market, because he does not know whether the architect needs how long time to build this house? So, this house building time can dominate the picture painter's acceptance of the architect's this free house picture product exchange offer, which is easier acceptance or difficult acceptance . In this six month' house building period between the architect service provider and the picture painter house buyer. Hence,the house building time can dominate the house building provider and the picture painter's house building buyer both's house picture free exchange purchase change behavioral choice between of them influentially.

The another time dominates consumption behavior case is that time rich or time poor factor, e.g. one fast food famous restaurant , its success is not only due to its fast food good taste factor, its restaurant location whether is close to the time poor people's offices, it is one main factor. Because this fast food famous restaurant only choose to build its restaurants to close to offices in any large cities in different countries. Hence, the franchisees need to pay expensive franchise loyalty income to buy its franchise in order to it can supply fast foods to the franchisees to sell, but they also need to pay expensive rent to this fast food franchiser, due to their fast food restaurant locations has been chose to locate in the main cities in different countries from the fast food famous restaurant's location decision. Hence, whether long or short time fast restaurant rent period to the franchisees , which can dominate the fast food restaurants's royalty and rent income. For example, if one fast food franchisee only sign one year contract to buy the fast food franchisor's loyalty to help it to sell its fast foods only one year, because it does not ensure how many fast food consumers will choose to buy these fast foods to eat, due to its price is decided by the fast food franchisor. If the cities have other fast food restaurants to let them to choose, they may find other fast food restaurants to replace it to eat fast foods very easily. If this fast good restaurant is not the most famous and it operates only short time. So, it can not earn more fast food franchisees‘ confidence to accept to pay long time rent to operate its fast food restaurants in cities and pay long time royalty fee to it. Otherwise, if the fast food restaurant had operated its restaurant for a long time period to raise its fast food loyalty's to let many different countries' fast food eaters to familiarize or acknowledg its fast food brand in popular. So, long fast food opersation time can confirm that it has many fast food eaters, they prefer to choose to eat its fast foods. It can increase the franchisees‘ confidence to choose to rent its fast food restaurants and pay royalty to it in preference. Hence, the fast food franchisor's restaurant operation time whether it is long or short time, this franchisor's fast food restaurant operating time pressure factor will dominate the fast food franchisees' choices to decide to pay how long rent sand franchise royalty income to rent its restaurant to do the franchisee's fast food business in the cities locations in different countries. So, it seems that the fast food franchisor's business operation time can dominate the frahchisees‘ choice.

In special , in fast food industry, time rich and time poor consumers behavior will dominate their fast food choices. Time rich people feel they have enough or too much time when time poor people feel time is a major constraint in their daily life. The explansion of the fast food business, and the increase eatting of fast food are indicators of this trend. At the same time, shorter working hours increased wealth and less pressure on domestic rountines have opened up new segments of leisure consumption. But, " free time" in certain areas has not for many people, lead to an increases feeling of time richness.

So, it explains that why many fast food consumers who feel not enough time to work daily. They are time poor working people usually. So, instead of fast food taste factor influences consumer number. The people who feel time rich or poor, e.g. employmet rich or poor lunch time to the employee, it will dominate the employee chooses to go to fast food restaurant in preference. So, the fast food restaurant can supply rich time to let them to eat lunch in short time, if the employee has less time to eat lunch or more tasks need hime to do on that day afternoon. Hence, feeling time rich or poor to the people factor, which will dominate some consumers' choices to some kinds of businesses, such as fast food industry, or for public transportation tool choice case example, one time poor passenger feels need to go to the destination in short time. The time poor passenger will prefer to choose taxi in preference, then it is possible train or underground train, next it is tram, fainally, it is bus or ferry public transportion tool choices. Otherwise, for one time rich passenger, he has more time to go to the destinaton. The time rich passenger will prefer to choose the cheap public transportation tool , such as bus, ferry, underground train, ferry, train. The final choice is taxi. So, passenger's time pressure will influence whose public transportation tool choice.

Is time pressure be the main dominiate to consumer psychological factor ?

What are the factors of time pressure dominate consumer purchcase psychological behaviors? How any why do this time pressure psychological factors dominate consumer behaviors? It is possible that time pressure can dominate consumer mind and behavior either choose to buy the product/consume the service or not buy the product/ consume the service. Every consumer's final purchase decision, he/she is influenced how to make by himself/ herself personal psychological limited time pressure . It means that he/she will have one time maximum standard to demand himself/herself to make the final purchase decision in whose individual psychological time standard (the consumer's individual psychological limited consumption time). So, it seems that ever consumer's final decision how he/she chooses to buy the product or consume the service, his/her consumption behavior will be dominated by whose psychological time limited consumption pressure.

So, time pressure issue seems evolutionary psychology, it looks at how consumer behavior has beed affected by psychological adjustments during time pressure evoluation. It seeks to identify which consumer psychological traits are evolved through adaptations, e.g. time pressure consumption adaptations to choose the final purchase decision in the final time limited consumption pressure environment, e.g. the consumer expects this day is the final day to choose to buy what kinds of the product. If he/she can't make final purchase decisin on the day, he/ she will choose to buy the kind of product later, even he/ she does not choose to buy the kind of product in the first or again, that is the products of natural selection, or the supermaket visitor case, he expects to choose which kind of food to eat within final 15 minutes, if he/she can't make the final decision to buy what kind of food to eat within final 15 minutes in this supermarket , or the restaurant eatting consumer case, he is queueing to wait to enter the restaurant to eat. He/she expects the final queue waiting time is 15 minutes maximum. If after this 15 minutes, he/

she can not be permited to enter this restaurant, then he/ she will choose to leave this restaurant and he/she will find another restaurant to replace it. So, it seems that any consumer will have himself/herself consumption limited stardard time to decide whether he/she ought choose to buy any products or consume any services in any consumption environment.

Hence, the cause of consumption time pressure dominates consumer behavior, it is based on these hypothesis: Every consumer has demand characteristic and time pressure can dominate how he/she make final decision to buy or not buy any product or consume any service as well as any consumer needs have time pressure consumption demand because he/she does not expect to epend more time to choose what kinds of products to buy or what kinds of services to consume. He/she expects to make purchase or consumption final decision in short time.

IN fact, consumers will be encoded to influence how they make final purchase decision. There are three main ways in which product information can be encoded. They include: Visual (product picture) ; for example, the conumer stores the memory by visualizing it as on product image. Aconstic (sound); here the consumer stores the information as a sound , this explains why some consumers sometimes get the brand name(words) that sound the same mixed up when they try to remember them. Semantic (meaning); here the object is stored in terms of what it means rather than as an image or sound, e.g. when the brand of toys can let many children feel fun to play. Then, when many parents feel familiar to the toy brand, they must remember this toy brand company is selling any kinds of toys to let children to play. So, famous brand can let consumers familiarize what products that it is selling. Such as the toy brand company can let parents feel its toys are fun to let their children to play. All these sensory information can dominate consumers make final choice purchase behavior to buy its product or consume its service in preference in any time limited pressure environment, if the brand can give positive information memory to let many customers to remember.

So, it seems that consumers are dominated to choose which kinds of products to buy or which kinds of services to consume by positive or negative emotion, time pressure in any consumption environment immediately. It is one time pressure consumption environment theory factor, it can influence consumer behavior is changed in any consumption environment time. Consequently, it explains that why time pressure can dominate consumer behaviors in possible. Also, any product seller or service provider needs to consider how to manage consumption time process to be longer to cause its consumers doe not choose to buy its product or consume its service consequently.

Can airport time consumption factor influence airport passenger shopping behavior ?

Instead of airport is one arrical and leaving terminal station place main function for any travelling passengers after the airplances had landed on the country airport's subway. I feel that airport has also another main functions. It can help the country to attract more travellers to choose to go to the country to travel as well as it can persuade them to raise consumption desire in their whole journeys after they leave the travelling country's airport if they feel the country airport's service performance can satisfy their short time staying need. I shall explain why any countries' airports can influence travellers' travelling destinations and travelling shopping choices to be increased or decreased.

The future airport will be the assistance role to assist tourim industry development. The factors include, for example, safety and terrorism control, when the travellers feel the country's airport is safe to stay when they catch air planes to arrive the coutry first time. Then, the country's airport can build safe image to let them to feel the country is safe to travel indirectly, traditional cirport service providers will need to seek new service way to deliver value, such as subscription based service models can let travellers to feel the country's airport can provide one comfortable and enjoyable short term travelling staying environment in the country's airport. Then, they bring pleasant emotion to prepare their journey trip after they leave the airport in the foreign country.

So, if the country's airport can let the travellers feel safe and comfortable , then it can bring new exciting and enjoyable feeling to the country's image. Because airport will be any travellers' first time arrival place after they catch airplanes to arrive another country. So, positive or negative airport's image will influence travellers how they feel whether the country , it is worth to choose to travel indirectly. However, airports need have good facilities to satisfy any related airplane service employees or any airport food or product businesses need, instead of travellers' need. For example, it needs have good allocation of terminals and access to facilities , they will be managed and regularly reviewed and regarded their good facility availability , capacity constraints and the best use of available facilities to satisfy any food or product sale shops' sale need and airport passengers' purchase need both in airports or airplane pilots, airplace service employees, irport security employees' comfortable working environment need.

However, airport inside and outside also needs to be arranged enough parking space facilities to let any aircraft parked or stored at the airport from the place where it is parked or stored in order to let any vehicles to be parked in airports or ouside airports easily and conveniently. When any sudden emergency matters occurred, the aircraft subjects to unforeseen operational delays , it should need to contact airport operations control centre to indicate when the expected time of arrival and departure is, there is no need to request a new slot in cases of unforeseen operational delays where the operation will take place within 24 hours of the agreed slot time. For example, of unforeseen operational delays include aircraft technical issues or weather conditions that could not have been planned for. Hence, operationally delayed aircraft must utilise slots in the same manner as originally agreed. If any change to the original slot agreement is required, e.g. a slot must be requested immediately. Moreover, when aircraft subjects to non-operational delays must request new slots immediately, following the correct process in those conditions of use, an example, of a non-operational delay may include delay caused by late running passengers or poor schedule planning. Hence, airport needs have good facilities and communication system to coordinate to any departments to avoid aircraft unforeseen delays to cause airport passengers feel nervous and brings negative and poor emotion to the airport's service performance.

On airport baggage handling function aspect, airport operators must comply with the baggage policy made available to all operators with the airline business management team. For example, where a flight destination or carrier is identified as being at significant or high risk, the operator will pay a charge as notified by management, equating to the cost of any policing cost additional to the services normally provided at the airport for carriers or destinations at lower levels of risk. In fact, airport baggage management needs be checked and delivered in order to help any airplanes' passengers to transport their baggages to follow their airplanes to be delivered to their same destinations when their airplanes are flying with the passengers and whom baggages to arrive the same country's airport at the same time absolutely. So, barrage management operators need submit or demand and in agreed format the already fleets absolutely, such as fleet detail to report these data to include aircraft type and registration, number of seats maximum take off weight kilogrammes of each aircraft owned or operated by the operator, in order to avoid any passengers' luggages wrong delivery occurrence in possible.

Hence, any airports must need to consider above basic passenger service operation in order to avoid any accident occurrences to bring poor airport service attitude feeling. If airport management expected that they have good service performance to satisfy travellers' short term staying needs in themselve countries' airport.

Any countries' airports expect to increase passenger movements, they must have effective strategies to carry on reviewing any errors and improve performance effectively. For instance, how to keep cost effective measures to lower operating costs and keep good performance on quality, such as for maintenance and cleaning airport cost reducing measures to introduce variable, performance -based elements to encourage productivity gains, how to manage and implement new technological systems to improve information flow and work processes within the country's airport, e.g. airport e-immigration system can allows to receive real-time alerts on any airport building faults. It can reduce airport reliance on manpower in these areas, thus reaulting in better productivity and cost savings for long term airport expenditure. So, high technological strategy system is needed to implement to any country's airport in order to facilitate the handling of more aircraft movements to optimise aircraft handling on runways. Their benefits include reduction of departure flights separation times, reconfiguration of flight routes, and improvements in runway inspection processes.

These new measures can bring effective in improving any country's airport's runway efficiency, developing new infrastructure including the extension of the taxiway, roadway and power supply networks. It aims to satisfy travellers' convenient transportation needs when they arrive any countries' airports and prepare to find suitable transportaton tools to arrive their destinations more easily (airport transportation roadway, taxiway building network strategy).

Hence, any countries' airports need have good strategy to manage a wide range of activities and risks, which are broadly classified into strategic , financial operational, regulatory and investment. Any countries' airports also need to seek how to reduce the occurrence of risks and to minimum potential adverse impact as much as possible, uch as airport risk management strategy. Because when the country has many people are living and they need often to catch airplanes to leave their countries to travel as well as there are many foreign travellers choose to travel the country. Then, the country's airport must need to expand size and raise good facilities, e.g. more automated immigration gantries are needed to be installed, taxi waiting areas are also needed to be explanded with additional taxi bays constructed to accommodate the higher number of arriving passengers , even increasing airplane subways number to satisfy many airplanes need to fly away from the country's airport or coming airplances fly to the country's airport's landing on runway needs often.

So, airplane subways number expanding strategy and cutomated immigration gate fast checking system is needed when the country has many travellers choose to go to the country travel and/or many local people need to leave themselves countries to travel. For instance, departure and arrival immigration control as well as pre-boarding security screening will be controlled for more efficient deployment of manpower and equipment. Moreover, in the line will the trend of self-service options of airports arrived the world, provisions will be made to have more kioslls for self check in,self-bag -tagging and self bad-drops. The increasing use of these options will help airlines and ground handling agents reduce processing times and staffing requirement. For example, a fully automated to reduce reliance on scare manpower baggage check in and check out system, the baggage handling system will also be equipped with ergonomic lifting aids to enable heavy and odd-sized bags to be handled with ease, even by older workers.

Then, the country's airport must need to increase subways number and immigration fast checking service facility to avoid handling passengers crowd queueing problem often occurs every day. When any airports often let passengers feel time pressure to queue to spend long time to wait immigration checks and leave the airport. It will bring their negative emotion feeling to the country's airport. Then, it is possible to influence they choose to go to the country to repeat travel again. Hence, the country's different airport strategies are needed when the country has increasing travellers number trend as soon as possible.

Another strategy concerns airport emergency service on safe aspect. Any countries' airports need have a highly trained specialist wait that is positioned to provid fast action rescue and fire protection for passengers' life safety ,e .g. aircraft rescue and fire fighting vehicles are needed airport. An incident command and control simulator which provides realistic and interactive simulations of emergency scenarios for the purpose of any sudden accident occurrences in any countries' airports.

So, any countries' airports need to develop an internal digital system to ease labour-intensive work processes like fire safety inspection, incident reporting, logistic management and recording of its personal fitness results, with the new safe system , data entry is needed mobile enabled with the use tablet computers. For example, the airport safe unit can continue to enhance its emergency preparedness and rescue capabilities with the successful staging of two drills, simulated aircraft crashes on land and at sea, as well as any exercises validated crisis contingency plans are recommended to earn strong capability in coordinating rescue efforts involving both the airport community and mutual aid agencies in order to carry on rescuing passengers and airport pilots and service attendants whom life safe service when air planes are crashed on land and at sea.

Another strategy is now aviation facilities strategy, it can support fly, cruise and fly-coach initatives, important options to a rising number of interm travellers, if it can be implemented successfully. It can bring enhancement measures benefits, includes the reduction of departure flight separation times, reconfiguring of flight routes and implementation of aircraft speed control for increased runway use efficiency.

Hence, one successful airport operation , the airport management needs to know how to implement the traveller check out or check in service functions when they arrive the airport or leave the airport and to satisfy its passengers' short term terminal station staying or transfering another airplane's flying need as well as it also needs to know how to implement its different strategies to improve its service performance and to let passengers have more confidence to the country's airport service operators' behavior and they also feel safe when they are staying the country's airport. Hence, any travellers' short term staying feeling in the country's airport , whether the country's airport can bring either positive or negative emotion , which will influence they choose to go to the country to travel again in possible. Hence, airport management can not neglect how to improve airport service performance to satisfy any first time or more time airport visitors' short term staying need.

Can web site online internet networking influence traveller individual behavior changes?

If web site can influence every online traveller user individual behavior change, how it influence every online user individual behavior change in order to impact his/her travelling service or arrangement change choice. For example, when the traveller walks in one travel agent's shop to find the most suitable travelling package for whose trip.

At the moment, he/she plans to find the travel agent to help him/her to arrange any travelling package. But when he/she goes back his/her home, he/she turns on his/her computer to link online travel agent website. Then, he/she discovers this online travel agent can provide more attractive travelling package similar service and he/she will compare the walk in travel agent's travelling package to this online travel agent travelling package. Although, the walk-in travelling agent can provide lesser service fee to compare this online travel agent. But , he/she feels this online travel agent can provide more attractive and enjoyable travelling entertainment and trip arrangement service to satisfy his/her travelling need. So, he/she decides to choose this online travelling agent's travelling package and it seems that the online travel agent web site can influence his/her original travelling agent target choice.

Nowadays, the most famous online development reshaping traditional marketing methods of tourism business will be possible to replace the traditional walk-in travel agent business. Because travelling consumers like to turn on computer to link to different travelling agents' websites to choose which travelling package is the cheapest or it can provide the most attractive or enjoyable entertainment arrangement in the trip. So, online travel agents will influence travelling consumers to reduce to spend time to walk in to visit any travel agent shops. The traveller prefers to spend much time to find which travelling agents' websites to find the most right online travelling agent to help him/her to arrange the trip service to replace to find the most right walk-in travelling agent at home conveniently. So, travelling agent website development can impact every traveller individual planning behavior to be changed influentially because when he/she plans to walk in to visit the identified travel agent shop, but when he/she has one desk top computer to be installed at home. Then, he/she will have another choice to buy the travelling package service. So, he/she will change his/her walk in to visit the travel agent planning behavior to change to clicking on any travel agent's website behavior.

Moreover, travelling website characteristics or attractive point is easy communication. When the traveller feels any worry or trouble, he/her need to enquire the online travelling agent immediately. He/she can send email to enquire the travelling agent to arrange travelling package similar service to walk in travel agent and he/she will compare the walk in travel agent's travelling package to this online travel agent travelling package. Although, the walk-in travelling agent can provide lesser service fee to compare this online travel agent. But, he/she feels that this online travel agent can provide more attractive and enjoyable travelling entertainment and trips service to satisfy his/her travelling need. So, he/she decides to choose this online travelling agent's travelling package and it seems that the online travel agent website can influence his/her original travelling agent target choice.

Nowadays, the most famous online development reshaping traditional marketing methods of tourism business will be possible to replace the traditional walk-in travel agent business. Because travelling walk-in consumer like to turn on computer to link to different travelling agents' websites to choose which travelling package is the cheapest or it can provide the most attractive or enjoyable entertainment arrangement .

Thus, online travelling information search tool can attract travellers to choose to find any travel agents' websites from internet to replace walk-in travel agents' shops influentially. Also, it seems online travelling service will be popular to replace walk-in travelling service in possible.

Every country cultural difference is different. How and why cultural difference has a real impact on tourist satisfaction and it can also influence to repeat travel. Is cultural tourism one major factor to influence tourist to repeat travelling intention or choice to the country in international tourism choice market? For example, China and India have similar culture. Their cultural difference is not much, e.g. eating cultural habit is similar , entertainment cultural habit is similar. These both countries people do not want to spend much money in eating and entertainment both aspects. Hence, these two countries people do not consider how to consume to enjoy entertainment and eat expensive food. Hence, it is based on cultural similar reason. These both countries tourists will prefer to choose to repeat travelling either China or India. When the Indian tourists had chosen to go to China to travel in the first time. Then, the Indian tourists will choose to go to China to travel in second time again. Also, the Indian tourists had chosen to go to China to travel in first time. Then, the Chinese tourists will choose to go to India to travel in second time again.

What factors influence China and India touists repect to travel between these both countries. The factors will include cheap air ticket price, cheap hotel living price , less economic cost factor. However, I believe the similar cultural factor will be the major factor to influence many Chinese and Indian tourist prefer to choose to repeat travelling between these both countries.

As my indication to these both countries people have similar eating habits, choosing foods, low health foods, common foods choice eating at cheap restaurant habitual consumption. Also, they have similar entertainment habits, their entertainment demad is not high. They like to ride bicycles to go to anywhere to travel. They like to go to swim, play backetball, football etc. sports. These all sports are cheap sport consumption. So, it based on similar individual low enjoyment demand and low health, food quality demand similar cultural factors. Chinese and Indian people have no long distance cultural difference between eating and entertainment habitual factor will include them to choose to repeact travelling between these both countries. Due to China and India have many restaurants can provide cheap food or sport service providers can provide diffent kinds of cheap sport entertainment consumption to satisfy their cheap food and cheap entertainment needs in their journey in China or India anywhere. So, it explains that why these both countries tourists will repeat to travel these both countries again after they had visited China or India to travel in first time. So, the similar cultural factor can impact these both countries tourists to repeat to go to these both countries to travel again. Hence, if these two countries' cultural distance is far or different, then themselves countries' tourists won't choose to repeat travel between themselves when these two countries for cultural distance toutists had visited to another country in first time. Hence, culture has been continuously considered as a much factor which tourists consider in terms of choice of the destination travelling place. Also, it explains cultural distance which can make tourist individual has less satisfaction to concern to tourists to repeat travels.

Otherwise, for far cultural distance two countries case example, such as Chinese and American , these two countries people's eating habit and entertainment cultural needs are different. For eating habit difference example, American like to eat poks, beefs, chickens, potatos to replace rice and other foods. Otherwise, Chinese like to wat rice, vegatables more than potatoes, porks , beefs for lunch , dinner . So , their eating habits are very different. Also, American like to drive boats on the seasor drive crs to go to anywhere to travel on holidays for sports or holiday entertainment activities . Otherwise, Chinese like to play backetball, football, ride bicycle of cheaper sport entertainment on holidays. So, American entertainment activities are more expensive to compare Chinese. Also, US and China , like families whose power distance is dfferent, such as every per family powerful member is parents, who have more power to give opinions to choose anywhere to travel for whose sons and/or daughters whole famlily members travelling arrangement.

Therefore, if the Us family powerful members, such as at least one son or/and ond daughter members who need t choose to go to which country to travel if the family powerful members, such as the child/ children's parent feel China's food taste or entertainment activities are totally different to be similar to their country's food taste and entertainment activities habitually after their whole fmily members had travelled to China in first time before.

Although, their son(s) and daughter(s) will hope to go to China to repect travel again. But, due to the US family parents are their son(s) and daughter(S) powerful decider to make any travelling decision to choose which country will be next time travelling destination. If their parents feel China's eating and entertainment culture is totally different to their countries. Then, the US family will not choose to repeat travel to the China country again any more easily, beause this US family can not feel satisfactory when they visited China in their first time before, due to they feel China 's food and entertainment cultures are totally different to their US country. So, the cultural distance factor will influence the US family don't choose China to fo repeat travel again.

Consequently, different countries' similar or different cultural factor will influence the country's tourists choose to repeact travel to the country again. So, any country needs to know what its culture is in order to attract the similar cultural countries tourists to repeat travel to itself country more easily.

Whether do different countries tourists‘ different lifestyle which can influence their travel consumption behaviors? Even, which countries that they will choose to go to travel. For example, when one tourist who owns himself/herself often to drive to go to anywhere habitually. The tourist's driving car habital behavior which will influence that he /she will feel need to rent car to travel to anywhere habitually , when he/she selects to go to the country to travel. Hence, if he/she feels the tourism destination has no any rent car service providers to provide him/her to rent any car to travel anywhere in the country's travel destination. Does the country lack rent car service factor which will influence that he/she will still choose to go to the country to travel in preference? For example, when one New Zealander's family who own at least one car at home. So, the New Zealand whole family every member can often drive car to go to anywhere , even, one family member had driven one car to leave his/her home. So, driving own car activity or behavior has been one habitual activity to influence the New Zealand every member to feel the travelling destination needs have rent car service provider supplies cars to let them to rent to travel. The driving car lifestyle has caused the whole New Zealander family driving habit. When the family's sons) and/or daughter(s) need(s) to go to school or go to shopping as well as their parents also need to drive their cars to go to office to work in themselves home town often. In common, there are many New Zealanders who will have at least one car at home because they feel that they can drive their themselves cars to go to anywhere in New Zealand more than waiting bus or tram or train or ferry etc. public transportation tools more conveniently. So, New Zealanders' driving own car habit will influence their lifestyle to feel that they also need to rent cars to travel to go to any where to travel to replace to wait public transportation tools choice in the travelling destination during their journey.

For shopping trips is more influenced by their driving car activities. So, it seems that this New Zealander families will be influenced to their tourism destination need, they need the tourism destination has car renting service provider to be supplied anywhere to let them can drive the renting cars to go to anywhere in tourism destination. It means that when the tourim destination has less rent car providers can provide renting car services to drive anywhere or it has none any renting car service providers are existing in the tourism destination. Then, the renting car service providers number shortage or none any renting car service providers to be provided to the country's tourism destination, which will cause the New Zealander families do not perfer to choose to go to the country to travel generally, e.g. Hong Kong, China, Korea these Asia countries have no many rent car service providers in these countries. So, the New Zealand families won't prefer to choose to go these countries to travel when they discover these Asia countries lack enough rent car service providers to let them to drive to travel in themselves conveniently. Otherwise, America, England, Japan etc. countries have many rent car service providers. So, these countries will be this New Zealander families' preferable tourism countries. Thus, the New Zealand families' driving ownership car lifestyle will influence their travel behaviors to choose to go to the country which can have many rent car providers in the tourism country any where tourism destinations in preference.

Thus, whether the country has renting car service providers , it will be variable factor to influence any country's car ownship families' driving car travel behaviors in their journey in order to let they feel that they can drive themselves ownship cars to go to anywhere to travel conveniently, even when they leave their countries. Hence, these countries' car ownship driving habitual families' behaviors will be influenced their tourism destination or location decision choice when the country has many renting car service providers in preference as well as this renting car service provider supplying factor will be more important to influence the habitual driving own car traveller to be preferable choice to compare other factors, e.g. cheap entertainment consumption providers factor which include cheap hotel living fee, cheap food price consumption etc. expenditure in the travelling country.

Thur, it explains that different countries' car ownship tourists , whose driving own car activities will cause their daily lifestyles, then their daily driving own car lifestyles will influence their tourism destination choices indirectly. So, it seems that lifestyle can be a outcome variable (or dependent variable) factor to influence travel behavior in any travelling built environment. The travelling built environment characteristics can include density measures (population density, job density), job-housing density). These travelling buit environment factor can repreent what the city resident's lifestyle. For example, where the location in relation to local centre or regional centre to the country's residents are living. This country resident's living location will cause this country resident's lifestyles , e.g. holiday or leisure whether it is low budget, active and adventurous or frequent traveller with second place or self-orgnized , family oriented or close to home and unadventurour. Hence, the country's living built environment will influence the country's resident's lifestyles. Due to different countries' residents will have different lifestyles. Hence, built environments and lifestlyes have relationship to influence every country's residents when they need to go to other countries to travel in their holidays. For example, frequent travellers are usually living in big and busy cities, otherwise, non -frequent travellers are ususally living in the countrysides, where there are less offices or factories are built to let people to work. So, big city will bring busy feeling to the country's residents, then they will be influenced to feel need to often to go to travel for leisure intention in their holidays. Otherwise, countryside will bring not busy or quiet environment feeling to the country's residents, then they won't feel working feeling when they are living in counryside. So, they won't feel need to go t o anywhere to travel in their holidays often.

Hence, built environment will bring either busy or not busy (quiet environment feeing) to the both different country residents when they are living in the places. Their living places will cause their lifestyles are different. Then, they will be influences to feel have more frequent travelling needs or less frequent travelling needs to explain why every country people will have more or less frequent travelling needs.

Printed by Libri Plureos GmbH in Hamburg,
Germany